The Spokane Aviation Story, 1910–1941

The
Spokane Aviation
Story, 1910–1941

by
James P. McGoldrick II
Former member Spokane Airport Board

Author of the *The McGoldrick Lumber Company Story – 1900 to 1952*

Revised and expanded from the 1982 edition
originally published by Ye Galleon Press
Fairfield, Washington

Tony and Suzanne Bamonte
P.O. Box 8625
Spokane, WA 99203
www.tornadocreekpublications.com

Copyright 2007, by James P. McGoldrick and/or Tornado Creek Publications
All rights reserved, including the rights to translate or reproduce this work or parts thereof in any form or by media, without the written permission of the author or publishers.

First edition, 1982
Second edition, revised and expanded, 2007
Printed in the United States of America
by Walsworth Publishing and Printing Company
Marceline Missouri, 64658

ISBN: 978-0-9740881-8-1

Library of Congress Control Number: 2007940044

Front cover photo:
Libby photo taken at Felts Field in 1927. A De Haviland DH-4 airplane, a 1928 Buick Roadster, and five guys having a good time.

Back cover photo: U.S. Air Force, wing commander, crew and J. P. McGoldrick, November 4, 1970.

Photo credits: Unless otherwise noted, all photos are from the author's collection. Photos credited MAC are from the Northwest Museum of Arts and Culture and photos from the Library of Congress are individually credited as such.

Tornado Creek Publications
P.O. Box 8625
Spokane, WA 99203
www.tornadocreekpublications.com

ABOUT THE AUTHOR

James Patrick McGoldrick II was born December 13, 1916, in Spokane. He was the oldest grandson of James Patrick McGoldrick, pioneer Spokane lumberman. From 1931 to 1935, Jim attended Lewis and Clark High School. In 1935 Jim was selected as the captain of the track team and, that same year, won the city and state champion high hurdles competition. He was the recipient of the Tiger Inspirational Award and also a member of the Crest Honorary Society.

From 1935 to 1940, Jim attended the University of Washington. During his college years, he was selected as captain of the track team. He was also the Pacific Coast Conference Intercollegiate champion of the high hurdles. In 1940 he was a National Collegiate Athletic Association medalist, a member of Phi Gamma Delta Fraternity, Spiked Shoe Club, Big W Club, Oval Club, and Fir Tree.

In 1939 Jim received Pilot's License #94032. He took his flight training at Boeing Field with Washington Aircraft Company (Elliot Merrill instructor). He spent World War II as a Civilian Radio Engineer with the Signal Corps, attached to the Air Corps.

In 1945 Jim started Northwest Electronics Inc., building it into a respected and successful electronics distributor and manufacturer. He was its president, C.E.O. and chief engineer until his retirement in 1981.

From 1964 to 1966, Jim was the chairman of the Spokane Chamber of Commerce Aviation Committee during the construction and dedication of the Spokane International Airport Terminal. From 1970 to 1971, he was the president of the Spokane Chamber of Commerce, and vice chairman of the Washington State Commission for Expo '74. During that same time period, he was also the director of the Expo '74 Corporation, and the trustee of St. Lukes Memorial Hospital.

Jim was an active private pilot and aircraft owner with land, sea and instrument ratings for more than 40 years. He has flown his own planes over much of North and Central America from the Pacific to the Atlantic and from Panama to Alaska. For 13 years, Jim commuted daily (in season) between Felts Field Seaplane Base and family summer residences on Coeur d'Alene and Pend d'Oreille lakes.

Jim has been a long time aviation authority and member of the old Businessmen's Pilots Association and the Quiet Birdmen. He is also a charter member of the Spokane Corral of The Westerners, a Northwest history organization founded in 1955.

In 1965 Jim was voted Spokane Pilot of the Year. He has flown various types of aircraft from an Aeronca Chief to a B-52. He has also flown numerous U.S. and foreign dignitaries, including congressmen, consular generals, USAF Division, Wing and Base commanders, visiting Chamber of Commerce dignitaries, as well as students and civil air patrol cadets. In 1987 he received the Annual Achievement Award from the International Northwest Aviation Council.

His wife Milaine and daughter Molly are also pilots.

Dedication

To my family's friend General Hillford R. Wallace (far right), who accomplished much and appears often throughout my book.

(Photo courtesy Wallace Aerial Surveys, South 163 Howard Street, Spokane, Washington, October 30, 1937)

Acknowledgements
1982

I am very grateful for the encouragement, help and material received from the following for the 1982 Edition: Gen. H. R. Wallace; Col. L. C. Sherman; Bill Toth; Bert Kemmery; Cip Paulsen; Caryl Lamb; Mrs. H. L. Budd; Thoburn Brown; Eric Anderson; Joe Stanton; Carl Partlow; Martin Seeger; Tom Mewborn; M. J. M. and T. Jones.

Also, my appreciation to the real recorders of "history in the making," the daily newspapers, whose old issues clarify the mind and provide for greater accuracy: *The Spokesman-Review*; *Spokane Daily Chronicle*; *Seattle Post Intelligencer*, and *The Spokane Press*. I also wish to thank God for photographers like Charles A. Libby and Son who had enough initiative and foresight to record the action and preserve the film that proves "one picture is worth a thousand words." Thanks also to the Northwest Museum of Arts and Culture for preserving and making so many of these photos accessible.

Acknowledgements
2007

I wish to especially thank Laura Arksey for her many hours of editing, researching, indexing, and the application of additional photographs from the MAC (Northwest Museum of Arts and Culture/Eastern Washington State Historical Society) to this project. I also thank Doris Woodward and John McGregor for their substantial editorial contributions.

Table of Contents

Introduction		.... page ix
Chapter I	The Early Days before World War I	.... page 1
Chapter II	The World War I Years	.... page 23
Chapter III	The Post World I Boom	.... page 33
Chapter IV	Our National Guard Squadron	.... page 55
Chapter V	The National Air Derby & Air Races	...... page 83
Chapter VI	The Tin Goose Era	.... page 133
Chapter VII	The Spokane Sun-God	.... page 148
Chapter VIII	The Airlines Cometh, Thank Heavens	..... page 161
Chapter IX	Other Pre-World War II Activities	.... page 174
Chapter X	Memorabilia and Miscellaneous	.... page 209
Index		.... page 235

INTRODUCTION

Much has happened in the field of aviation in this world of ours since the Wright brothers made their historic first powered flight at Kitty Hawk, North Carolina, in 1903. The growth and progress in the art of flying and the flying machine, during the lifetime of many of those still among us, has been one of the most remarkable stories of achievement of modern mankind. Many times I have thought to myself, "What a privilege to have been born during this almost unbelievable era." For centuries man has longed to "fly like a bird" and yet it has only been within these relatively recent times that thousands of persons, from all walks of life daily ride the magical jets back and forth between centers of commerce, or on happy vacation trips, with an unassuming nonchalance that would have staggered the imagination of the richest king on earth less than a century ago!

Most of us take this routine experience more or less for granted. I think a little reflection on and appreciation of those early days can only increase the significance of this rewarding experience of being able to fly like no human has ever before.

I am sure most of us feel history is interesting and educational. It is my conviction that local history is even more so. With this in mind, and with hope somebody else, young or old, might be interested, I have brought together a collection of Spokane aviation memorabilia that otherwise might be forgotten with the passing of time. Hopefully, it will serve to document those golden years so that future generations might have the knowledge of how it all started and be able to share in the satisfaction of human progress.

Why me? Why should I undertake the challenge? Well, I have lived in Spokane for more than 90 years and have been interested in aviation since the early 1920s. My father, Milton T. McGoldrick, knew many of the young men and women who made the earliest local aviation history, and he and his friends passed on much of the happenings through the years. Then I and other pilots and aviation boosters of the next generation carried the story forward.

I apologize for not being able to complete a second volume, as I had hoped, to bring the history up to present day. However, this covers an era in which many of the old timers have "gone west."

The Early Days Before World War I

The front page of the Sunday morning March 27, 1910, *Spokesman-Review* announcing the introduction and coming arrival of the first airplane to fly in Spokane.

Spokane's First Airplane Flight

The "Flying Machine" began making history in Spokane in 1910. The March 27th edition of the *Spokesman-Review* announced: "Charles K. Hamilton, the famous aviator, who will give exhibitions of his skill at the Interstate Fairgrounds April 1, 2 and 3 will arrive in Spokane this morning from Vancouver, bringing his Curtiss biplane and accompanied by his manager, Nat Reis, and two machines."

Charles Keeney Hamilton
The First Man to Fly an Airplane in Spokane

A promotional photo of Charles K. Hamilton, circa 1910, and a *Spokesman-Review* ad announcing Spokane's first upcoming aviation meet. *(Photo courtesy Library of Congress)*

Charles Hamilton was born at New Britain, Connecticut, in 1885. In 1903, at the age of 18, he became active in hot-air ballooning and parachute jumping at circuses and fairs. In 1906, he teamed up with Roy Knabenshue and the two of them began piloting dirigibles. By 1909 his daring flight exhibitions throughout the United States made him perhaps the best known American flyer at that time. Known as a daredevil pilot who would fly anything anywhere, Hamilton repeatedly crashed his *Hamiltonian*, a biplane powered by an eight-cylinder engine. During the same year, he became an exhibition pilot for Glenn Curtiss Airplane Company. In June 1910, he participated in the Dominguez Field Air Meet and won a $10,000 prize for flying from New York City to Philadelphia. In October of that same year, he flew at the New York International Air Meet. He was also credited with the first documented night flight, which took place over Knoxville, Tennessee.

By this time, many in the United States had grown tired of just watching aircraft fly. Hamilton responded with what were then considered daredevil antics. People were convinced that if the engine stopped, the machine would crash; the idea of gliding was still only vaguely comprehended. One of Hamilton's first and very successful stunts was to climb to some 1,500 feet above the exhibition grounds and cut his engine. He would then dive steeply, pulling out at the last possible moment, then land. The public loved his skill and bravado. A number of other pilots, in attempts to copy Hamilton, plunged to their deaths, thus proving the actual risks Hamilton was taking. These risks were very rewarding financially. A pilot could earn as much as $10,000 for two or three flights of 10 or 15 minutes duration – a large amount of money in 1910.

The following year, Hamilton joined Moissant's International Aviators, a group of flyers who toured the United States performing daredevil exhibitions, hawking barnstorming flights and reportedly earning $100,000 a year. During a performance with the group in El Paso, Texas, he flew over Ciudad Juarez and observed engagements between the Mexican militia and rebels, which is one of the earliest recorded uses of an airplane for military purposes.

Although Hamilton's aviation career was undoubtedly spectacular, it was cut short on January 22, 1914. At the time of his death, he reportedly had two replaced ribs and metal plates in his skull and one ankle. Hamilton is buried in the Cedar Hill Cemetery in Hartford, Connecticut. His burial records state he died in New York City. He was almost 29 years old. The cause of death is listed as fractured ribs.

A promotional photograph of Charles K. Hamilton sitting in a Curtiss biplane, circa 1910. *(Photo courtesy Library of Congress)*

The Promotion of Spokane's First Air Show

On December 17, 1903, Wilbur and Orville Wright of Dayton, Ohio, became the first to solve the problem of controlled powered flight in what they called a "Flying Machine." Although they received a patent from the United States Patent Office on March 14, 1903, it wasn't until the fall of 1908 that their accomplishment was generally accepted following their first public flights – Orville at Fort Meyer, Virginia, and Wilbur in France. From that date forward, the concept of aviation burst upon the world with an unstoppable impatience. The spark that was to be the beginning of the airline industry was ignited. Throughout the nation, men were scrambling for a piece of this new, exciting and daring industry. There was money to be made and great fame to be gained.

In Connecticut, as in the rest of the country, the flying fever gripped the imaginations of such men as Charles Keeney Hamilton, Nels J. Nelson, Frank Payne, George F. Smith, Peter Dion, Howard S. Bunce, Christopher Lake, Percival Spencer, and others. Shortly after the Wrights' flights, these men took to the skies in backyard manufactured flying machines similar to the Wrights' but different enough to avoid patent problems. Charles Hamilton was among the first. He quickly gained fame for to his skill and courage. He was in demand across the nation, being sought out for exhibitions in almost every large American city – the competition for Hamilton was fierce.

On March 21-26, 1910, Spokane hosted an "Automobile, Aeroplane and Motorcycle show" at the Princess Rink with the famous Curtiss biplane on exhibit. However, it was not flown. Following that event, there was a promise that aviator Walter E. Donnelly would fly the Curtiss, but that fell through.

During the time promises were being made and broken by others, Harry Green, a Spokane businessman and promoter, arranged for Charles Hamilton to appear at the Spokane Fairgrounds for a three-day aerial exhibition to be held April 1-3, 1910. Green, often referred to as the "The Duke of Spokane," was born on August 10, 1863, at Prenn, in Poland. He came to America in 1878 at the age of 15, moving to Texas, where he lived for 13 years. In 1891 he relocated to Spokane, where he became one of the city's better known business men, investing in property and stocks. However, his biggest contribution to Spokane history was as a promoter of sporting events and entertainment. In 1900, he purchased a one-half interest in the Club Cafe in Spokane. For several years he owned a racing stable, often entering his horses in the big stakes offered by the Oakland, Los Angeles, Portland, Seattle, and Spokane racing associations. His horse Royalty was the winner of the Seattle and Spokane derbies of 1903. He often traveled to California where he became well known for the heavy bets he often placed on his favorite horses. In 1902 he purchased an interest in the Spokane Northwestern League Club and, as the result of his efforts, gave Spokane one of its best and most popular baseball teams. He also became interested in the theatrical world through his close friend, John Considine, of Seattle. Green owned stock in the Orpheum and the Washington theaters of Spokane and also Vancouver theaters. He was a promoter of boxing contests and the owner of one of the finest dog kennels in the Northwest. However, Green's biggest contribution to Spokane was his introduction of the airplane. He was assisted in this promotion by Lew Berg, a semi-silent partner.

Harry Green
(Spokane and the Inland Empire by Nelson W. Durham, 1912)

Green died at the Ridpath Hotel on December 14, 1910, following a brief bout with pneumonia, only nine months after his introduction of aviation to Spokane. He was survived by his wife Emma, adopted daughter, Helene J., three brothers, an uncle, and a cousin.

CHAPTER 1 – THE EARLY DAYS BEFORE WORLD WAR I

The 1910 Air Show

Day one, April 1:

On April 1, 1910, the first day Charles K. Hamilton was scheduled to fly, he was unable to get the motor running on his Curtiss biplane. The following day the *Spokesman-Review* headlined an article: "Biplane Engine Balks." Hamilton also ran the following ad:

> # Hamilton Explains No Flight
>
> ## Engine Freighted Upside Down—Oil in Magneto—All Right Today.
>
> "I was much disappointed this afternoon when my engine failed to work, as I fully intended to make my flights according to schedule despite the wind and rain. The engine trouble was due to the fact that in shipping the engine had been allowed to stand wrong side up and the oil had run out of the crank case into the magneto, which necessitated the thorough cleaning of that machine.
>
> "My cases are marked properly, so that they should be kept right side up in shipment, but in this case the directions were not followed. In order to repair the damage to make my flights tomorrow it is necessary to take the magneto apart and clean it with gasoline, which we will do tonight and tomorrow morning, so as to be ready on schedule time tomorrow afternoon.
>
> *Chas. K. Hamilton*

Day two, April 2:

Spokane's first airplane flight took place on April 2, 1910. The following article appeared in the *Spokesman-Review* on April 3, 1910, the day after this historic Spokane flight:

> Despite inclement weather and threatened rain, aviator Charles K. Hamilton made two successful flights at the fair grounds yesterday afternoon. The first flight, made at 3:11, lasted about five minutes, during which Hamilton traveled about three or four miles through the air and circled the racetrack twice in front of the grandstand. In this flight he started from the southwest end of the center field in order to rise into the wind blowing from the northeast.
>
> After running along the ground for about 100 yards at about 40 miles an hour the machine and its aviator rose into the air gracefully and the first aeroplane flight to he seen in Spokane was on, with cheers from the spectators. As soon as he got above the ground about 20 or 30 feet the wind carried him east at the rate of about 50 miles an hour. At this distance from the ground he circled several times, gradually rising to a height of 200 or 250 feet above the earth, at which height he twice circled above the track, covering the half mile in 43 seconds.
>
> He circled the track twice when he cut off his engine, landing from the north end of the center field, running southward along the ground and stopping a few feet east of the tent used to house the biplane.

Crowd Cheers the Aviator

As the machine left the ground first a few feet at a time and then faster as the machine gained headway, the crowd of several hundred people in the grandstand set up a big cheer for the first aeroplane to fly successfully in Spokane. After the first flight everyone crowded around Hamilton to shake his hand and congratulate him on his success.

The second flight was even more successful than the first, lasting about seven minutes. In this flight the aviator was forced about a mile or a mile and a half east of the fair grounds where he circled over the houses before being able to get back over the grandstand. While east of the grounds Hamilton found a high-power, 12,000-volt electric line in his path. Being unable to rise sufficiently to pass over it, he let his machine run a few feet above a street, passing below the wires and between the poles, he ran along the road for quite a little distance before being able to get above the wires and in the clear sufficiently to soar.

When he disappeared from sight on this flight to the east of the paddocks everyone feared that something had happened but the sharp cracks of the engine could be heard as he regained altitude and hove again into sight above the track.

Has Remarkable Control.

On his return from the second flight he passed across the center field at a height of about 15 feet to allow the *Spokesman-Review* photographer to get a good view of the machine and aviator in the air. When asked to fly low for the purpose Aviator Hamilton asked, "How low do you want me to fly? I can take the hat off your head if you want me to, for I can fly any height above the ground." This shows the remarkable control of the machine which he exercises and which allows him to traverse the air wherever he pleases.

After descending from the second flight, Aviator Hamilton decided to give it up for the day and make his preparations for today's flight which will include the complete program as announced for Friday. Yesterday the engine worked fine, never failing, and starting on the first turn of the propeller.

In order to get the machine in shape for the flights yesterday and those today Aviator Hamilton worked late Friday night on his magneto. He found it necessary to buy a new one to replace certain parts of the magneto damaged by oil. In order to do this he offered to buy Harry Green's automobile for $3,500, it being absolutely necessary to have a six-cylinder magneto.

Only Eight-Cylinder Biplane.

Green refused to sell his car at the price named so Hamilton got a six cylinder magneto from a new automobile which he adapted to his eight-cylinder engine. His biplane is the only Curtiss machine in the world equipped with an eight-cylinder engine, and it is the same machine as used at Rheims, France, by Glenn H. Curtiss, the rudder still bearing the number 6 which the machine carried at the meet.

The crowd which assembled at the Fairgrounds yesterday was agreeably surprised when the management announced that no tickets would be taken up, but that those would be good for the meet today, when the full program will be carried out unless it rains pitchforks, and in any case Hamilton intends to make a flight. After his flights yesterday Aviator Hamilton said:

Ground Good for Flying.

This ground is very good for flying, affording a good start and landing place, but everything is surrounded by a network of electric wires, which makes it a rather dangerous pastime in case my engine breaks down while I am too far away to land on the center field. It also is pretty cold this kind of weather, for when going through the air I make about 50 miles an hour. I do not wear gloves unless absolutely necessary, as it spoils the sensitiveness of my hands in handling the vertical and horizontal rudders.

Aviator Hamilton is always smoking a cigarette, and before each flight he always lights a fresh one to smoke while in the air. He smokes all the time, even when around the engine or gasoline cans, whether the cans are open or the gasoline is being vaporized by the engine.

The only extra protection he wears while in the air is a leather coat, and the only reason he wears this is because in an accident last fall his leather coat saved his life by preventing one of the broken stays of the machine from piercing his body. It also saved him a hard knock several weeks ago when he took another fall from slight altitude.

While the altitude of Spokane is pretty high, about 2000 feet, it is not the highest place at which I have used my biplane," said Aviator Hamilton last night. "At El Paso Texas, about 3500 feet above sea level, I had to increase my plane surface nearly twice until the total spread of my machine was 47 feet. It is now 27 feet. This makes the machine too hard to handle to practice at lower altitudes though it of course gives a greater lifting power.

Altitude Affects Flights

The altitude greatly affects the aviator, as he can not fly only so many feet above the sea level with a given size machine. With this machine I have here I can fly 3600 feet above sea level, or about 1600 feet at Spokane. Another thing which has to be changed with the altitude is the inclination of the rear rudder plane, which affects the speed with which I leave the ground. This only can be set by trial, so my first flight today was not as satisfactory as it might have been, the rudder having too slight an inclination for this altitude.

While in the coast cities I had excellent weather, in fact this is the first bad weather I have recently struck. While at St. Joseph, Mo., I flew while it was three degrees below zero, at which temperature I had to wear gloves, which I never do unless it is very cold. It was pretty chilly today, as the speed with which I go through the air literally drives the cold into a person.

Aviator Hamilton standing by his plane smoking a cigarette. (Photo courtesy Library of Congress)

Day three, April 3:

Hamilton's final day in Spokane drew an estimated crowd of 20,000, although only admissions for 3,000 people were collected. In a *Spokesman-Review* article the following day it was stated:

> The number of persons who saw Hamilton fly would be hard to estimate with any degree of accuracy. ... on roofs of houses and factories, in tree tops and on telephone pole crosspieces and standing outside the enclosure in throngs of thousands upon thousands, the crowd was practically innumerable. Every eminence that appeared above the fair ground's fence within the view of the grandstand was black with people.

At the end of this three-day event, the following was revealed in the *Spokesman-Review*:

> **Spokane Date Costly**. One feature by which Spokane was given the Hamilton exhibition of the last few days came to light yesterday, when a series of telegrams between Glenn H. Curtiss and Hamilton, the former in Hammondsport, N.Y., were made public. It was shown that because Hamilton insisted on flying in Spokane, the Curtiss interests had to pass up a contract at Memphis, Tenn., and New Orleans, La., that Curtiss wire says, cost the company at least $25,000 ... Curtiss demanded that Hamilton cancel his Spokane and Seattle engagements and Hamilton refused.

"Mechanics, helpers and boys are shown getting the machine into a position for the second ascension. The airship is too large to be taken through the gate at the fairgrounds." *(1910 Spokesman-Review photo & caption)*

Aviator Hamilton (fourth from left) next to his airplane at the Spokane Fairgrounds. *(Photo courtesy Spokane Public Library, Northwest Room)*

On April 3, 1910, the following article appeared in the *Spokesman-Review* below this photo: "Aviator Charles K. Hamilton making flights in his Herring-Curtiss biplane at the fairgrounds yesterday afternoon. The picture at the left shows a rear view of the aviator and his machine as it flew past the photographer at the rate of 50 miles an hour. On the right is a view of the machine taken as the aviator was swooping to the ground to make a landing. In landing, the aviator lets his machine gradually settle to the ground, along which it runs on a set of three wheels. The lower picture shows the biplane running along the ground on making the flying start. This machine differs from the Wright model in starting under its own power and without any special starting mechanism. While in the air the machine travels at a rate of about 50 miles an hour and on the ground the speed is from 25 to 45 miles an hour." *(1910 Spokesman-Review photo and caption)*

Hamilton racing an auto on the Galveston Beach, circa 1911. *(Photo courtesy Library of Congress)*

A 1908 Dirigible Exhibition in Spokane
The forerunner to the Airplane

A dirigible at the Spokane Interstate Fairgrounds in 1908. At the time of this photo, the fairgrounds was located between Sprague on the south, and Springfield on the north, and Altamont and Regal on the east and west. Although much of Spokane's history has recorded the first fair in Spokane as being held at Corbin Park, it actually was held on Spokane's South Hill. According to a 1886 *Spokane Falls Weekly* it was held from September 21 to October 19 in 1886, and, according to the 1887 *Spokane Falls Directory*, the location of Spokane Falls first fair was at: "Washington Fair Association (Francis Cook Pres.), grounds one mile south of city." It was only at the South Hill location for one year. The following year, 1887, it was moved to Corbin Park, and in 1901 it was moved to the above location off Altamont. In 1930, the fair was temporarily discontinued. In 1934, Playfair was organized and leased the grounds from the park commissioners for use as a horse racing track. This proved compatible because when the fairground off Altamont were originally built they included a one-half mile racetrack.

The word dirigible come from the French *dirigible*, meaning "steerable." The first airships were called dirigible balloons. Over time, the word balloon was dropped from the phrase. The "Golden Age of Airships" began in July 1900 with the launch of the Luftschiff Zeppelin LZ1. The zeppelins were named after Count von Zeppelin who began experimenting with rigid airship designs in the 1890s. At the beginning of World War I, the zeppelin airships had a framework composed of triangular lattice girders, covered with fabric and containing separate gas cells. Multi-plane, later cruciform, tail fins were used for control and stability, and two engine/crew cars hung beneath the hull, driving propellers attached to the sides of the frame by means of long drive shafts. Additionally, there was a passenger compartment (later a bomb bay) located halfway between the two cars. *(Photo courtesy Shelly Ruff, Merel Stoddard albums)*

CHAPTER 1 – THE EARLY DAYS BEFORE WORLD WAR I

Cromwell Dixon
The Fatal Event in Spokane of the Nation's Youngest Pilot

Another significant local happening to ignite the interest of the young men of my father's age group was the appearance of a 19-year-old pilot named Cromwell Dixon Jr. at the Spokane Interstate Fair on Monday, October 2, 1911. This daring young man from Columbus, Ohio, had become nationally famous only two days before by being the first person to fly across the Continental Divide of the Rocky Mountains. He flew his Curtiss Pusher from the Helena Montana State Fairgrounds westward across the divide to Blossburg, Montana, and returned. (A fire was lit in Blossburg to create smoke to guide him to his destination.) It is said, "Dixon fought 30 miles per hour winds for 20 minutes before gaining enough altitude for the return trip, but finally made it over to receive a hero's ovation from the record State Fair crowd and a proclamation from Governor Edwin L. Norris as the greatest aviator in the world." He won a prize of $10,000 and a spot in the history of aviation for this accomplishment.

Unfortunately, in the process of his taking off from the infield of the Spokane Interstate Fairgrounds (later Playfair) "a gust of wind" caught his plane, plunging him to his death on the railroad tracks just north of the racetrack. Pictures of the wreckage show the damage to the Curtiss and where "his horribly mutilated body" was found in the wreckage.

It is a sad page in history when a young man becomes famous, and rich, and dead, all in a span of three days! There was a favorable side to the event however, as a number of local enthusiasts had again seen a flying machine, reinforcing the local interest in aviation aroused the previous year with Charles Hamilton's appearance in Spokane.

It is interesting to note that Cromwell Dixon Jr., born July 9, 1892, was then the youngest licensed aviator in the world. His License #43 was issued August 31, 1911, by the Aero Club of America and he had been flying for only two months. A bronze plaque at the Helena Airport commemorates Dixon's flight and a forest service campground on MacDonald Pass is named for him.

The newspapers of the day further reported that another young pilot, Robert St. Henry, and Curtiss aircraft were a part of the same show at our fairgrounds. The two were to alternate their performances and on the following day, St. Henry went on to continue the show. During his performance, he accidentally landed his plane on the roof of the grandstand with little damage to himself and the plane.

The appearance of young Dixon and his associate at the fair was not unusual for the times. It is easy to visualize just about how this happened. In the June 8, 1911 issue of *Aero – America's Aviation Weekly*, numerous advertisements proclaim: "Do you want to be an Aviator? All pupils entered are graduated with Pilots Licenses – the best of equipment insures graduation in shortest possible time – Spring Class opens April 22, 1912 – good positions to capable Aviators – The Glenn L. Martin Co., Box 222, Los Angeles, California."

The General Aviation Company Aviation School of Boston brags about its "competent instructors," the fact that "students may receive instruction in Burgess-Wright and Curtiss-Type biplanes and Hydro Aeroplanes," its "Aviation field with 10 mile level course with adjoining Hydro-Aeroplane Station," and its "four courses of instruction (1) Regular Flying (20 lessons), (2) Cross-Country Flying, (3) Shop Course (build and repair), and (4) Apprentice Course, "and no charge for breakage."

This highway marker honoring Cromwell Dixon, is located on MacDonald pass where U.S. Highway 12 crosses the Continental Divide west of Helena. There is also a mural depicting the historical flight painted by Montana artist Robert Morgan in the terminal building at the Helena airport.

The $10,000 prize Dixon won for being the first person to fly across the Continental Divide of the Rocky Mountains had been raised by a consortium that included John Ringling of the Ringling Brothers Circus and, Jim Hill, the president of the Great Northern Railway.

The fairgrounds at Helena, Montana, located at 4,000 feet above sea level, served as Dixon's ramp to the Divide. It took him 15 minutes to reach 7,000 feet, which was 800 feet higher than the mountains he was to cross. Guided by the smoke signal set by the people of Blossberg, Dixon cleared the crest of the Divide near Mullan Pass, where wind currents reportedly flipped his airplane upside down. Recovering, he landed in a field one mile from the railroad depot and 18 miles from Helena. The entire flight took 34 minutes. Two days later Dixon died in an accident in Spokane.

Hearing of Dixon's death, people in Helena raised money for a memorial in Dixon's name. The marker was dedicated in 1912 and placed at the point where Dixon made his celebrated landing. *(Bamonte photo)*

These two photos taken on September 30, 1911, make a visual record of Cromwell Dixon, the first aviator to fly across the Continental Divide. The caption on the upper photo states: "First Airship Crossing Continental Divide Sept. 30-11. Cromwell Dixon – Aviator. Start for [from] Helena." The caption under the lower photo reads: "First Airship Crossing Continental Divide Sept. 30-11. Cromwell Dixon – Aviator. Landing at Blossberg, Mont. from Helena, Mont." *(Photos courtesy Library of Congress)*

THE MARTIN AVIATION SCHOOL, Los Angeles, Cal.
Do You Want To Be An Aviator?

All Pupils entered are graduated with Pilots Licenses
The best of Equipment insures graduation in shortest possible time

Spring Class Opens
April 22, '12

Special inducements to first ten pupils entered

Send today for
Illustrated Catalogue

Wire entry for Spring Class

MARTIN AVIATION SCHOOL
GOOD POSITIONS TO CAPABLE AVIATORS
Aeroplanes, Hydroaeroplanes and Accessories
DON'T OVERLOOK THIS PROPOSITION
THE GLENN L. MARTIN COMPANY,   Box 222, Los Angeles, Cal.

An ad from the June 8, 1911 issue of *Aero – America's Aviation Weekly.*

Under the heading of "Directory of Aviators" (which is for the benefit of county fair managers) we see: "The American Aviators, Inc., now booking exhibitions with Wright Aeroplanes and Burgess Hydroplanes," similar ads for "The Curtiss Aviators" of New York, "National Aviators" of Chicago, and "San Francisco Aviators," along with a number of individual flyers are all listed as available for exhibitions – "If they don't fly, you don't pay!"

The same magazine has the "Scale Drawings of the New Curtiss Racer" (in case someone wanted to build their own) and numerous interesting technical papers on aeronautics by well-known experimenters like E. R. Armstrong, Gustav Eiffel, J. W. Mitchell and others.

The seven issues of *Aero and Hydro* given to me by Bert Kemmery, from his boyhood library of aviation which guided and motivated him to an early experience in aviation, document this era better than anything I have seen. A reprint of these issues would find great interest in today's airplane buffs, but since this is a "Spokane Story" I would leave these jewels of wisdom for another time. Suffice it to say, young boys like Dixon learned to fly in a few hours, probably listed themselves with a booking agent, and went out into the world to find fame and fortune. Some did.

Plans for "how to build a new Curtiss Racer" from *Aero – America's Aviation Weekly.*

Cromwell Dixon's pilot's license

Cromwell Dixon's last exhibition flight. He was killed two minutes after this photo was taken.

Cromwell Dixon's fatal crash site. These photos were taken immediately following his tragic death.

CHAPTER 1 – THE EARLY DAYS BEFORE WORLD WAR I

The year 1912 saw some activity among the would-be flying enthusiasts. A man believed to be R. C. McClellan, a Ronan, Montana, balloonist and parachute jumper, had built a Curtiss type pusher craft and had about four students he was hoping to teach to fly. In 1963, at a Spokane Chamber of Commerce Aviation Committee banquet celebrating the 70th birthday of General Hillford R. Wallace, I had the privilege of interviewing Bert Kemmery of Spokane. Bert was a friend of my father (as was Hillford Wallace) during those school boy days and was one of the four original students of McClellan. Bert related how he and Deb Wylie, B. C. Smith and another chap had first started their training "at a field just east of the Fairmount Cemetery gate" and west of what is now the Veterans Hospital. In this level field paralleling the road that became a part of the Joe Albi Stadium south parking lot, he had his first "instruction." This consisted of "sitting in the aircraft and driving down to the end of the field several times." He related that the first time he got enough nerve to pull back on the controls and get off the ground, in his panic to get back on, he made a hard landing, and damaging the aircraft which required repairs.

The following year, operations were moved to a "field out by Parkwater" where the first activities on what is now known as Felts Field began in 1913.

My father, who as a boy had lived at East 930 Boone Avenue (near Hamilton Street), told me during my adolescent years how "one of the boys in the neighborhood had built an airplane and later flew it himself at a field out near Parkwater." He said the young man, Deb Wylie, accompanied by a large group of kids, had taxied down the field a number of times to get the feel of the machine. As the ground was rather rough and the craft quite fragile, it was necessary occasionally to warm up the blow torch and solder the leaks in the radiator before the next try. This was done while the kids looked on in hero admiration and fascination.

One day, after several trial ground runs (the story goes), Deb pulled the aircraft off the ground and "flew to another field some distance away," much to the astonishment of those shouting young observers in attendance. The way I remember the tale, the "other field" was Fort Wright, but this was not so.

In a taped interview, Bert Kemmery gave me a more accurate accounting of the occasion. He was there, as was my father and his brother Ed. Firsthand accounting is much better than "hand me down" tales. The aircraft was, of course, McClellan's Curtiss pusher and the "other field" was probably Orchard Avenue, one mile east, rather than Fort Wright, several miles west. (This illustrates how history has a way of getting a little mixed up as it passes through the generations.)

Another more momentous 1913 flight Bert described was the "first circling flight by a Spokane-trained aviator." Up to this time most of the training flights were in a straight line from one field to the other. On this occasion, Deb Wylie told his associates that "this time I am going to make a turn." After a normal take off at Parkwater, Deb flew east about a mile as he had done several times before. Instead of landing there, he disappeared from view over the trees and the crowd became alarmed, fearing he must have crashed.

Bert and several others jumped on the running board of my Uncle Ed's National racing car (Ed was one of the few older boys who owned an automobile and was active in auto racing at this time), and they proceeded eastward along the south bank of the river through the rocks that separated the two fields, expecting to find a crumpled airplane somewhere over there. They had not gone far from Parkwater, when to their joy and surprise, the Curtiss appeared just behind the trees flying down the Spokane River upstream from the dam and landed back at the starting place. Spokane flying activities had begun in earnest.

Hillford Wallace and Dad had recalled to me that Deb Wylie was a chauffeur for A. F. McClaine. McClaine's son Fielding was married to Maude McClaine, one of Spokane's first and most attractive female pilots and a friend of my parents in the late 1920s and 1930s. I remember her flying an open biplane at the Mamer Flying Service at Parkwater.

The *Spokesman-Review* on Sunday, October 23, 1973, carried a historic picture with a caption: "Flying Machine Roars off Field in Downtown Spokane." It went on to say, "This print had been made from an old-time glass plate found in an antique shop by Norman D. Hackhalter of Spokane." It shows a Curtiss pusher airplane taking off from Glover Field, which used to be our main athletic field in the early days and was located just west of the Spokane Club parking lot on the south side of the river. The article states: "Several of the pusher type of Curtiss planes were demonstrated in Spokane, Sandpoint and Coeur d'Alene in 1911 to 1914." (Incidentally, this is the place I saw my first track meet between Lewis and Clark and North Central high schools in the early 1920s.)

In this picture the not-quite-finished Monroe Street Bridge is in the background as are the terminal of the electric Interurban railroad, the Washington Water Power office building, and the tower of the old Auditorium Theatre building which stood on the corner of Main and Lincoln. The wood ramp on the south end of the concrete bridge is plainly visible and it is interesting to note this remained for many years due to the lack of stability of the fill.

When you think that the field is scarcely 100 yards long and tucked tightly into the river bank, this is really quite a feat even for our modern aircraft, let alone a 1912 kite! As yet I have not been able to find who made the flight or took the picture; however, by an extreme coincidence I learned in a conversation with Lorin Markham, former manager of the Spokane Chamber of Commerce, that he remembered this flight, having seen it as a very young man. He also stated that the plane after taking off from Glover Athletic Field circled and flew under the Monroe Street Bridge (from east to west) as a part of the same exhibition.

Curtiss Pusher type aircraft taking off from Glover Athletic Field, circa 1912. *(Courtesy MAC, Frank Guilbert photo L96-35.64B)*

The same aircraft coming upstream to land at Glover Field, completing the stunt that reportedly had it also flying under the Monroe Street Bridge (not confirmed).

And finally, I ran onto another photo of the same plane flying east coming up river to land at Glover Field. Those were the days.

While we are on the subject of Glover Field, I have had remarks from both General Wallace and Al Connick inferring that Nick Mamer did a similar stunt in the early 1920s. Both of these stories had Nick flying over the Spokane Falls to give his passengers a good view, when suddenly his engine failed and he had to land in the river near the same spot. Some doubt regarding the credibility of the "emergency" status of the landing is brought forth by the fact that a photographer was said to just happen to be on hand to record the deed.

I have not been able to uncover much substantiating evidence of this later feat other than a comment by my friend "Bud" Allen (formerly of the old Palace Department Store and later The Crescent) that he remembers seeing the plane partially in the river near Glover Field after the emergency landing. At first I thought it was possible that during the years the two stories have been confused and the 1913-1914 incident is the only one. However, it is now evident that the second happening, years later, did occur, although not quite the same as originally described.

About the same time, on the other side of the river, my two cousins, Glenwood and Stanley Lloyd, who then lived at the end of Mallon Avenue just across from St. Luke's Hospital, recalled how they watched an old-style plane land in the field between the railroad tracks and Broadway Avenue. The pilot stepped "out," and hired one of the biggest kids gathered there to watch his plane while he walked over to a girl's house to have dinner or something. This must surely prove that the airplane in that day did actually have some utilitarian use and was not just for stunt performances at local fairs.

This photo of an airplane just prior to flight in Spokane contained the following narrative: "Early aeroplane at Glover Field along the south side of the Spokane River, just west of the Monroe Street Bridge. *(Courtesy MAC, photo L96-35.72B)*

By comparison, a similar situation in Chicago described in a 1912 *Aero Weekly* tells how Farnum T. Fish was forced to land in Grant Park when the adverse winds prevented him from continuing his flight to Milwaukee. The reception committee there consisted of two park policemen who promptly placed him under arrest and took him to the station, where he was later released under a $400 bond. He protested the city ordinance as being inadequate, saying he was forced to land to save his life.

Another Chicago pilot was "booked" when he unknowingly broke the city ordinance by flying from the Aero Club field at Cicero to the Columbia Yacht Club to keep a luncheon engagement. Somebody is always trying to take the fun out of life! (Even then it was better out West.)

During those few years before the entry of the United States into World War I, flying machines were starting to appear almost everywhere here in our country and in Europe. The movie many of you may have seen, *Those Daring Young Men and Their Flying Machines*, entertainingly characterizes this period.

Typical were occasions when one of the local daredevils or a famous barnstorming pilot and auto driver would appear at the fairgrounds and race each other around the track with the plane at low level, much to the amusement of the crowd. The stunt was done throughout the country and happened in Spokane on July 15, 1915, when the then famous Barney Oldfield (cigar and all) raced De Lloyd Thompson in the Curtiss.

The *Spokane Daily Chronicle* told the story:

> Although he did not fly quite so high as he did Tuesday afternoon, when his biplane collapsed, Aviator De Lloyd Thompson gave the 3,000 people who gathered at the Interstate Fairgrounds Wednesday plenty of thrills. Thompson was in the air for 12 minutes on his first flight of the day. The wind was blowing about 20 miles per hour and he went

Bert Kemmery's wife found this photo of her husband sitting in the cockpit of this traction monoplane in about 1915. The plane is undoubtably the one built by Arthur Arneson and is a copy of the French Bleriot XI design that Louis Bleriot first flew from France to England in 1909. (Both had a three-cylinder air-cooled 30-horsepower Anzani engine) The aircraft was a step forward in design and popular before WWI. The plans were probably published in Aero & Hydro Magazine **and followed by numbers of amateur builders. Also, I am sure that the damaged wood prop I had seen for years on my grandfather's garage on Rockwood Boulevard, which was put up on the brick wall by Uncle Ed, was from this plane. It was this same design and had a couple of inches missing on one blade. I'm sure it was a memento cherished by aero collectors.**

> through his usual performance of looping the loop, doing the corkscrew glide and the undertaker's drop. Thompson's second flight which included his race with Barney Oldfield, the noted auto speeder, ended in his simulation of a war aviator, dropping bombs on a miniature fort. Thompson literally ran away from Oldfield in this race, the auto speeder having no chance to keep up with the aviator.

Incidentally, my mother and father witnessed a similar performance while attending the Pan Pacific Exposition (World's Fair) in San Francisco in 1915. I think the airplane always won.

Shortly after the early Curtiss Pusher era in Spokane, a good example of the enthusiasm and ingenuity of local craftsmen is brought out by an undated copy of an old news article with headlines that read, "Spokane Man to Attempt Flight in Monoplane He Built Himself." A picture shows Arthur Arneson standing beside a handsome tractor propeller type of monoplane which he built in a garage at South 218 Brown Street during the previous winter, probably 1914, and which he hoped to fly "early this spring." It was reported that "every part of the machine was made here with the exception of the engine which was a French Anzani 30 Horsepower. It has ample power, Mr. Arneson states, to carry the big bird anywhere." (The Anzani was a three-cylinder air cooled design.)

> The clipping goes on to say: "The Aerial craft is 34 feet from tip to tip of wings, and 20 feet in length to the tip of the tail from the propeller. It has 198 square feet of spread and weighs 360 pounds without the rider. Mr.

Levi Hutton on the left in an early vintage biplane. *(Courtesy MAC, Hutton Settlement collection, L94-24.351)*

Arneson's weight is 153. He will make the first flight in the machine the latter part of April or early May. The builder of the Spokane monoplane is not new at the work as he has built three other machines that have been more or less successful." (He apparently survived them.) "The Spokane monoplane is the best I have ever built," Mr. Arneson stated, "and I am positive that it will be a successful aerial craft. We will make the test when weather conditions are favorable."

Incidentally, this particular clipping was sent in to Joel Ream of the *Spokesman-Review* by a man in Kimberly, B. C., who said he found it in his mother's trunk and wanted to know if the pilot made out OK. Some further information regarding the engine appeared in the *Chronicle* on January 15, 1920, which stated: "A feature of the exhibit will be the Anzani French type air-cooled engine which propelled the first plane over Spokane about seven years ago. The plane, a monoplane, was built and flown by T. L. Thompson and Arthur Arneson of Spokane, who are regarded as the pioneers of the Northwest in Aviation." Of course the article is not completely correct in saying, "The first plane over Spokane." More correctly it was the first tractor monoplane built in Spokane, and furthermore the T. L. Thompson mentioned was undoubtedly the same De Lloyd Thompson who raced Barney Oldfield around the fairgrounds' track and possibly the one who flew the Curtiss from Glover Field. He was undoubtedly Spokane's most prominent flyer in the years just before World War I. Arneson may have done most of the building and Thompson most of the flying. One thing for sure, this must have been a milestone in Spokane aviation history.

Chapter II

The World War I Years

In preparation for going to war in 1917, aviator William Thompson stands beside an airplane at the U.S. Aviation School in Ashburn, Illinois. This photo was taken when very few of the airplanes were armed, although the pilot carried a pistol. *(Photo by* Chicago Daily News *photographer, courtesy Library of Congress)*

Early in World War I in Europe, the airplane had a minor status indeed, its chief value at first being only for observation. Soon somebody up there in the wild blue discovered another airplane next to him that apparently belonged to the "enemy," and he pulled out his pistol and pointed it at the bounder. From there all hell broke loose and planes were designed with machine guns aboard to knock the opposition out of the sky, for dropping explosives, for reconnaissance, puncturing observation balloons, strafing columns of men and equipment, and many other destructive assignments.

Back home, the United States hoped we wouldn't get involved, but undoubtedly had a feeling we probably would. At first, we helped the "good guys" with supplies. A short article in the Spokane paper in 1917 advises: "Spokane Dirigible Builders Plan War Machines for U.S.," and it goes on to say:

> Will speed construction of Flying Craft – McGoldrick offers Facilities. Dirigible aircraft may be constructed for Uncle Sam in Spokane within 30 days. Preparations to start operations are being made by the Harvey-Campbell Dirigible Aircraft Corporation of Spokane, according to an announcement made today by Earl G. Harvey, President. A number of Spokane men are being interested in the new enterprise. "In case of war our lumber yards and facilities will be at the disposal of this aircraft company," said J. P. McGoldrick, President of the McGoldrick Lumber Company, today. "I am not interested in the company at the present time, but I am favorably impressed with what I know of it and I may be interested later on."

The company had capital stock of $1,000,000. The incorporators were Earl 0. Harvey, O. A. Campbell, A. E. McGoldrick (Uncle Ed), Kenneth Campbell, and W. B. Riddle.

Mr. Harvey goes on to say:

> Our first craft will cost about $4,500 and will have a carrying capacity for six passengers. We hope to develop the speed of 45 miles per hour. The machine will be of the non-rigid type, 110 feet long and 32 feet in diameter at the widest point. It will be the stream-line construction combining the features of the aeroplane and balloon. I have had a great deal of experience in the building, operation and flying in all manner of aircraft, having been in the business for 20 years. In California, we built craft that with a 22 horsepower engine gave us 35 miles per hour. I have made various improvements and applied for patents on them. With these and with a 70 horsepower eight cylinder engine that I will use, I expect to get a speed of 45 miles per hour.

Another newspaper release announces:

> The Inland Empire will furnish the United States government a squadron of airplanes if an aviation camp is established at some point near Spokane, according to a plan announced today by J. C. Argoll, chairman of Mayor Fleming's committee to establish a camp. Eight men have enrolled in a class in dirigible building and operation being organized by Harvey-Campbell Dirigible Aircraft Corp. Those enrolled are E. A. McGoldrick, Thomas A. Wall, Ralph K. Cline, Willie E. Lang, Kenneth Campbell, A. M. Fredericks, Arthur J. West and Roy E. Metcalf.

Finally, Mr. Harvey is quoted: "I expect to leave for San Francisco within the next few days to purchase a suitable engine and equipment for the first machine." Just what happened to the idea, or if Mr. Harvey came back from California, I don't know. Maybe the United States was brought into the war unexpectedly soon and the plans had to change. Anyway, we did not build dirigibles in Spokane.

When the Germans sank the *Lusitania* in 1917 and the United States was brought into the war completely, much change occurred almost overnight. The country was wholeheartedly dedicated to doing everything it could, as exemplified in America's best-known WWI song "Over There," written by George M. Cohan. Part of the lyrics to this song included: "get it over – over there." As a result of numerous efforts thousands of young men began volunteering for the various services. Consequently, the country became hard pressed to design, build and activate all the necessities of war. These included airplanes, lots of airplanes, mostly for training.

The plane decided upon for the primary trainer was the Curtiss JN-4, popularly called the "Jenny," with the Curtiss OX-5 engine. It had a span of 43 feet, length overall of 27 feet, and an empty weight of 1,430 lbs. Maximum allowable gross weight was 1,920 lbs. which gave a useful load of 490 lbs., of this the fuel (21 U.S. gal) was 130 lbs., oil 30 lbs., pilot 165 lbs., and passenger 165 lbs.

The OX-5 engine was a 90-degree V-8, with a 4-inch bore and a 5-inch stroke with push rods and open rocker arms for the overhead valves. With its long stroke, it was "red lined" at 1,400 RPM and developed 90 horsepower at that speed. It consumed nine gallons of fuel per hour and drove the "Jenny" at 75 miles per hour maximum with a landing speed of 45 miles per hour. Construction was mostly of wood and fabric and several factories in the United States and Canada turned out the craft. The Canadian model was known as the "Canuck."

The secondary trainer chosen was the British-designed De Haviland DH-4. This ship was a little larger, heavier and much more powerful. It had the newly designed Liberty V-12 engine which had been developed in a short period of 90 days by an engineering team led by Packard and Hull-Scott. It was produced in numbers by U.S. automobile factories. This brute of an engine had a 5-inch bore and 7-inch stroke for a displacement of 1,650 cubic inches (27 liters) and developed its 400-plus horsepower at a low RPM, about 1,500! The Liberty had separate water jackets around each individual cylinder, with a tubular overhead cam shaft on top of each bank. Exhaust came out the outside of the 45-degree V while intake manifolds were inside with the carburetors. Fixed-pitch wood propellers were utilized.

Most of the U.S. manufactured DH-4s were used for advanced instruction, although they were designed for firing machine guns through the prop forward, and with a turret on the rear cockpit with twin Lewis 30-caliber guns for protecting the aft quadrant. Only a few actually got to the front and were not highly regarded there because they were quite heavy.

Instruction for the flyer recruits was at a number of fields, but Kelly Field in Texas was then the place to go. About the time the United States aircraft industry got into high gear, the Armistice was signed on November 11, 1918, and the war was fortunately over.

The reason I bring up the Jenny (JN-4) and the DH-4 here rather than the planes that actually flew in combat, such as the British Sopwith Camel and SE-5, the French S.P.A.D. and Neupert 17, the German Fokker Triplane, Fokker D-VII, Albatros and Pfalz, is that the former were the only ones we saw in Spokane in this half dozen years after the Armistice.

Of the many Spokane men who joined the U.S. Army Air Corps and the Navy and received training in aircraft, I can only recall a few personally that were friends of Dad's. I know there are many more, but after all, I was born in 1916 and missed out on this period. Tom Symons, Bill Barnard, Jack Fancher, Ed Wirt, Hillford R. Wallace and Floyd McCroskey presently come to mind.

It is interesting to note that General Hillford R. Wallace, whom I knew most of my life and was very close to until his death in 1985, got his start in aviation as a result of World War I. "Wally," as he was affectionately called by his many friends, was a boyhood chum of Dad's. (They shared their first bachelor apartment together and I'll bet they were able to get into plenty of trouble.)

Although he figures prominently in future chapters, this is a good place to document Wallace's early history. Wally started life in an unusual way, born January 21, 1891, in a Pullman car stranded in a snowstorm outside of Fargo, North Dakota. His father was a Canadian who ran a clothing store in a small town that was a Canadian Pacific Railroad division point between Calgary and Banff National Park. His mother was from Morris, Minnesota, and since he was her first, she was on the way home to have her baby. "Old Man Winter" changed the plan somewhat, but everything turned out fine. He later had a sister whose daughter married Col. Robert Smith, and then a younger brother. After a few Canadian winters, the family moved to Spokane, where Wally attended Logan and Bancroft elementary schools. He then graduated from North Central High School about the same time as my mother.

General Wallace's distinguished military career began during World War I as a 1917 volunteer in the Signal Corps. He was stationed at an aircraft acceptance base rear Glasgow, Scotland, as a mechanic. As an enlisted man, he often flew with a pilot and occasionally was privileged to bring the plane back by himself, thereby gaining some flying experience. He liked flying so much he applied for flight training, but the war ended before he was accepted.

After returning home for a short time, he was ordered to report to Kelly Field in San Antonio, Texas, for flight training, and in nine months graduated as a second lieutenant in the Army Reserves. In 1920 he returned to Spokane and didn't get a chance to fly much until 1924 when the 116th Observation Squadron of the Washington Air National Guard was formed. Wallace was one of the 13 original officers. During this period, he also helped to put on the 1927 National Air Races and Air Derby in Spokane.

Wallace attended the Air Force photographic school and from that point on, he specialized in aerial photography, both in his military and civilian aviation career. In 1938, as a major, he was appointed commander of the 116th Observation Squadron of the Washington Air National Guard. During World War II, he served as deputy director of Air Force reconnaissance, organizing training for photographic operations. Under his command, the 116th Observation Squadron produced thousands of aerial photographs that are still very useful for historical research in this area. In 1948, as a brigadier general, he was appointed commander of all guard air units in the Spokane area, as well as commander of the National Guard 60th Air Force Wing, which included fighter groups and squadrons in other cities. It was quite a rise from enlisted man to brigadier general.

General Hillford R. Wallace. *(Courtesy MAC, Libby photo L84-256.56, Mamer-Shreck Collection)*

Wallace's civilian career was no less significant for Spokane aviation. In 1937 he formed Wallace Aerial Surveys, Inc. to provide aerial photographics for the Department of Agriculture. This became Wallace Air Service and Wallace Aeromotive, which he sold in 1964. He remained very involved in civic and National Guard activities during this period.

Aviation and World War I Enlistment Drive Posters

This poster depicts a soldier holding a wrench and waving to an airplane in flight.

It also includes a list of occupations available, such as chauffeurs, wood workers, auto mechanics, photographers, motorcyclists, and opportunities for 40 other trades. *(Courtesy Library of Congress, LC-USZC4-7558.)*

A U.S. Army Air Service recruiting poster showing men on an airfield with airplanes flying overhead, and six illustrations of classrooms for the welding department, motor transport department, practical drafting, blueprint reading, instruction in areo engines, an ignition course, and machinists' practice shop. *(Courtesy Library of Congress, LC-USZC4-7556.)*

A 1917 World War I poster depicting two soldiers, one using binoculars, in foreground, and an American airplane above. *(Courtesy Library of Congress, LC-USZC4-5869.)*

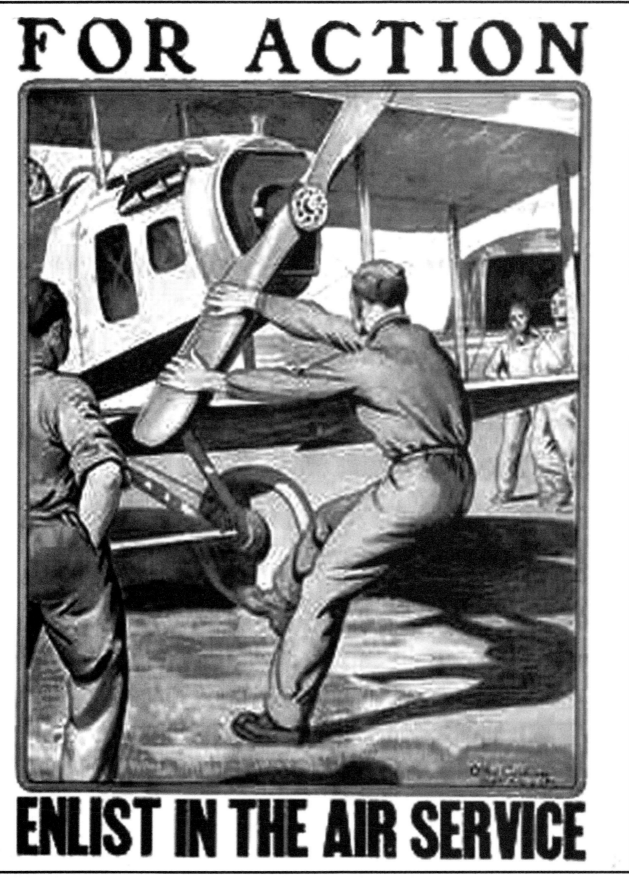

A 1917 U.S. Army Air Service recruiting poster showing soldier cranking an airplane propeller. *(Courtesy Library of Congress, LC-USZC4-7559.)*

Two soldiers in front of an airplane, 1919. *(Courtesy Library of Congress, LC-USZC4-5870.)*

This 1917 recruiting poster showing soldiers, an airplane and airships around the USA star insignia. *(Courtesy Library of Congress, LC-USZC4-7594.)*

World War I
National Photos

This photo taken October 15, 1918, at Frankfort, New York, is of a Langley night bombing airplane. *(Courtesy Library of Congress, LC-USZ62-100390)*

An example of the nation's fascination with aircraft and its application to the military. This photo was taken at Love Field Aviation Camp, Dallas, Texas, May 30, 1918. *(Courtesy Library of Congress, Frederick W. Hellenberg photo)*

Chapter III

The Post World War I Boom

A rare night shot of a "swinging crowd" in 1920. The aircraft is a three-place Curtiss Oriole. *(Photo courtesy J. Walt Davis)*

The period following World War I was marked by a vigorous growth in flying activities around the nation and in Spokane. The young men who were given flight training by the government, and released from the service before they got into actual combat overseas, naturally wanted to continue to fly and to get into aviation when they came home. Also, the large fleet of training aircraft the government had rushed to build were now considered largely surplus and were to be sold. This combination of circumstances provided the ingredients for a substantial surge in flight activity.

The first mention I can find regarding aviation activity in Spokane after World War I appears in the *Spokane Daily Chronicle* on February 13, 1919:

> The Northwest Aircraft Company of Spokane has leased from the City Park Board 1,000 acres of land at Parkwater, east of the city, for a period of three years. The deal closed yesterday. The land is to be used for hangars and training grounds. The first trial flight of planes now under construction will take place within the next three weeks between Spokane and Lewiston. One between Spokane and Tacoma will take place within four weeks, it was stated today. Within the next 18 months two passenger planes will be operating between Spokane and Seattle, according to plans. Each plane will be capable of carrying 12 to 14 passengers besides the pilots, and will make the flight in four and one-half hours. Spokane is to be the hub of a Northwest air service that will in the next few months make it possible to have breakfast in Butte, luncheon in Spokane, and dinner in Seattle. The announcement made this morning by officers and representatives of the company.

This is probably the most overstated claim I have ever heard! If you took it literally, it would imply that it was possible to organize, design, build, test and start operating an airline from scratch in a matter of a few weeks. Naturally, it didn't happen that way. However, the year 1919 did mark the start of the postwar period of aviation progress in Spokane.

The *Spokane Daily Chronicle* continued the story with a release dated April 21, 1919:

> Because of hazards both to spectators and aviators the War Department has ordered that the flying circus must discontinue staging its exhibitions and stunts directly over municipalities. Orders received late last evening by the advance representatives for the flying circus make it necessary for the exhibition to be held somewhat away from the main part of the city, where spectators may have an opportunity of protecting themselves against danger. The flying circus management therefore announced that the exhibition which will be given by the planes Wednesday will take place directly over Parkwater.

On April 25 the paper reported:

> Four Curtiss biplanes sweeping majestically into the heavens in perfect formation, officially opened Spokane's flying circus at Parkwater this afternoon. The exhibition began promptly at the scheduled time of 1:30, with weather conditions almost ideal for a most successful display of battle airplanes. As the planes swung gracefully over the crowd estimated to be 20,000 people, great quantities of Victory Loan literature were dropped. Just as the American planes made their first circle over the flying field, the little German Fokker ship rolled sharply and took off in hot pursuit, starting the great mid-air battle which is the feature of the flying circus. The papers which the American planes dropped were in the shape of bombs and bore this inscription. How many Victory Notes would you be willing to buy if these were German bombs? Victory and Liberty Notes paid for peace.

On June 5, 1919, a blurb in the paper recounted:

> Miss Spokane (Marguerite Motie) will christen her namesake, the first airplane of the Northwest Aircraft Co. of Spokane, at a formal ceremony at Parkwater the latter part of next week, it was announced today by Treasurer R. C. Steeple. The plane, which has been named the *Miss Spokane*, will be christened in the presence of city officials, the representatives of the Ad Club, the Chamber of Commerce and other civic bodies and guests of the company.

Next we hear of the actual christening in the June 14th issue of the *Chronicle*:

> Dedicated to the beginning of a great industry, the first Spokane made airplane [they had forgotten about Arthur Arneson already] was christened *Miss Spokane* by Miss Marguerite Motie, the original Miss Spokane, before a large crowd at Parkwater Aviation field this afternoon. The airship was given its appellation when Miss Motie cast into its whirling propeller a beautiful bouquet of sweet peas, red roses, canterbury bells and fern leaves. Lt. Clyde Pangborn, the aviator, then flung off into a graceful exhibition of the machine's maneuvering power passing the spectators each time so near the ground that they could plainly distinguish the workmanship of the machine.

This is interesting because it tells of Clyde Pangborn for the first time. He was raised in the St. Maries, Idaho, area and went on to become famous in aviation circles mostly because of his 45-hour flight from

Tokyo, Japan, to Wenatchee nonstop in October 1931. He had intended to complete his flight in Spokane but belly-landed in Wenatchee instead. He was, according to a press release in the 1970s when he was awarded the Honor of Membership in the "OX-5 Club" (posthumously), "the Chief Pilot for the Veteran Spokane Airman, R. C. McClellan, who had built his own demonstration airplane." He was also famous as a stunt pilot, popularly referred to as "Upside-Down Pangborn."

Now enters the "guy" about whom we hear more later in this year 1919. The June 20th issue of the *Chronicle* announces:

> The Cascade Mountains today were crossed by an airplane for the first time. The first time this feat has ever been accomplished was by a Spokane man, Lt. J. M. Fetters, formerly a dancing master here. He was accompanied by Sgt. Owen Kessel, who has been with him on his flight from the Army Aviation field at Mather Field, Sacramento, California, where both men are stationed. Lt. Fetters made his takeoff from Seattle at 10:01 o'clock this morning. One hour and ten minutes later they were over the big range of mountains and had landed at Cle Elum. Later in the afternoon they intended to fly to Ellensburg and Yakima. The flight of the aviator is in the interest of Army recruiting in the state. From Yakima they expect to fly to Pendleton, Oregon and Walla Walla tomorrow. Saturday noon they will start for Spokane.

This is all part of the story, because later in the year "Jay" Fetters brought two Curtiss JN-4 aircraft to Spokane that he had purchased surplus in Texas, according to Al Connick in a taped interview in 1964. Al, a young man at that time, described how he had helped assemble the planes that had been shipped on a flatcar to Parkwater. They flew them several times before disassembling and storing them for the winter.

Also, a report again in the *Chronicle* dated August 24, 1919, states:

> Spokane is to have another passenger airline service. The new service will be during fair week by Lt. W. T. Barnard, formerly a member of the United States Army Aviation Service. The plane, a two passenger JN-4D, was selected from the Mather Field training ship being sold by the government at Sacramento, California by Lt. Barnard's brother, N. N. Barnard, who is also an aviator. A temporary tent hangar will be used for the ship and arrangements are being made for a landing field near the city, probably on a paved road. We will be prepared to take passengers anywhere at any time, said Mr. Barnard this morning.

By this time, you can see that things were starting to move in Spokane aviation circles and the September 19th *Chronicle* indicates the need for some kind of regulation:

> Declaring the situation at the municipal flying field at Parkwater, under three year lease to Northwest Aircraft Co., to be anything but favorable to the advent of further planes flown by Spokane men, the Spokane Flier's Club at the noon luncheon today unofficially announced itself as favoring action through city officials which would seek to clarify the situation. Members of the club expressed themselves as heartily in favor of the establishment by the city of rules and regulations governing the field at Parkwater and of municipal laws regulating aircraft traffic.

From this statement one can only guess that two problems had emerged. One was that the field was under lease to the Northwest Aircraft Company, which expected to manufacture aircraft there and very possibly did not want other operations on the field. I suspect this because other landing areas were being developed, as we shall see. The other was that the pilots were apparently "feeling their oats and kicking up their heels" so much that some kind of authority was needed in the interest of safety.

Also, on September 1, 1919, the *Spokane Daily Chronicle* states:

> The first moving picture of Spokane from an airplane will be taken late this afternoon, when A. L. Trado of the Alexander Film Co., flies over the Interstate Fairgrounds and the downtown section of the city in the Curtiss plane piloted

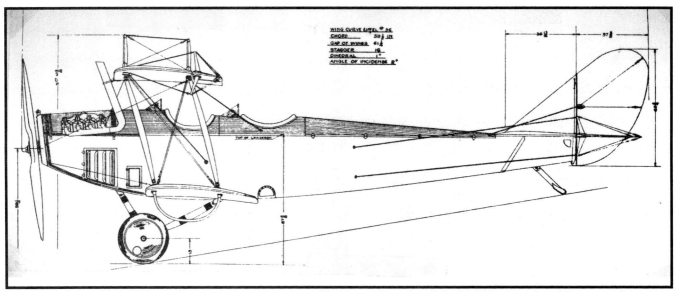

The Curtiss JN4-D "Jenny" was designed as a military trainer for World War I and sold as surplus after the Armistice. With so many planes available, the manufacture of postwar designs was handicapped. One of the planes popular in Spokane was the Lincoln-Standard. Like the Jenny, it had a longer upper wing, with ailerons and, in my mind, was not as graceful as the Jenny, with its positive stagger and declining line of thrust.

by Tom Symons. A feature of the picture will be the employment of a gyroscopic device, the invention of Trado, which eliminates the vibration of the machine and produces a picture as steady as those taken from the ground.

On the lighter side, the October 6, 1919, *Chronicle* tells that:

Flying in formation yesterday, with Miss Helen Burns, daughter of Mr. and Mrs. Edward Burns [they lived just north of the Sacred Heart Hospital on eighth Avenue] and Charles O'Ferrell, son of Mrs. James Breen, as passengers, Lts. Bill Barnard and Paul Frances finished a flying trip by staging a miniature air battle. Barnard's *Liberty* [an error] was slightly damaged three weeks ago (see reference to loose cowl strap) and Frances carried his passengers in a Canadian Curtiss [a "Canuck"]. They remained in the air 30 minutes over the east end of the city doing a series of stunts, one plane remaining directly over the other while the aviators exhibited a number of fighting tricks. During the afternoon, a dozen passengers were carried, several of them on stunt flights.

With the coming of winter, the flying activities slowed down a great deal. The decade of the 1920s, however, did get off to an early start when the January 15th *Chronicle* announced the following event:

The first display of airplanes by an agent in the Inland Empire, and probably in the Northwest, will be seen in Spokane during the Automobile Show when the Symons-Russell Aviation Co. will exhibit its famous Blue Bird JNP-4 Curtiss plane at the Ahrens and Ahrens showroom. The Symons-Russell Co. has in transit several new planes, but will exhibit the Blue Bird as a sample of its stock of machines. The display will be limited by the small space allotted to the aviation company, but educational features as used at the school of Symons-Russell Co. east of the city will have a prominent place. A feature of the exhibit will be the Anzani French type air-cooled engine which propelled the first plane over Spokane about seven years ago, etc. [See previous remarks about Arthur Arneson in 1913.]

As spring arrived in 1920, other things started to happen in Spokane aviation.

Actually, two flying fields were being developed at the same time, only a mile apart: one at Parkwater and one a mile south on East Sprague, the old Appleway. In the local newspaper dated March 15, 1920, a headline, "Spokane Aviation Co." told about "three former army pilots and a first class civilian mechanic had formed the Spokane Aviation Company, which intended to do all kinds of commercial flying and

Having fun at Parkwater in 1920.

A Curtiss JN–4, possibly belonging to Bill Barnard or Jim Fetters.

also conduct a school for student aviators. William (Bill) Barnard (Spokane), Sam Stenstrom and Dave Matthews from Moscow, Idaho, are the flyers and Nathan Barnard will handle the mechanical work," the article declares. "The Company already has the JN-4's and proposes to buy a three seater in a short time. Construction of a four-place hangar has already been begun on the municipal landing field at Parkwater, just outside the city limits. Passenger carrying work has already begun."

Bill Barnard, incidentally, was a friend of Dad's, and I remember hearing about him when I was a kid. I had the pleasure of talking to Bill in the late 1960s when he was visiting in Spokane. He told me how in 1919 he had purchased a used JN-4 trainer for what he remembered to be $4,500. According to Bill, in the fall of that year he took off from Parkwater and was embarrassed to find he had not fastened the leather strap that held the engine cowling in place. The wind flapped the strap and buckles so violently that he was forced to make an immediate landing, and in avoiding the crowd gathered that Sunday, damaged the aircraft somewhat. Although repairs were made, his wife had a heart-to-heart talk with him, and as a result, he eventually and reluctantly gave up his flying activities.

Bill's brother "Nat" purchased a new JN-4 Curtiss that year for only $3,500 and continued to enjoy flying for some years. These two prices mentioned seem a little high to me, because Lindbergh said he only had to pay about $600 for his "very used" Jenny that he flew a short time after this.

Personally, I remember Bill Barnard best when he was a Plymouth/Chrysler dealer at Third and Howard, west from the Central Methodist Church and "kitty-corner" from Vic Dessert's Pacific Hotel in 1931.

I can remember driving to Liberty Lake with my parents in the early twenties and seeing the Symons-Russell Airport just north of the tracks with its east-west gravel strip runway and the hangar with several aircraft parked there. Tom Symons and his family were neighbors of ours at Liberty Lake. He was a charter officer of the 116th Air National Guard Squadron and of the World War I training era. He was married to one of R. L. Rutter's daughters and their son, Tom Jr., and daughter Gina grew up with us at the lake.

Tom was the owner of the Symons Building on Howard between Sprague and First in Spokane, and was of additional interest to me, because he was the owner of a pioneer radio station KFPY (KXLY) then housed in the Symons Building (I was also a radio enthusiast at an early age).

On April 24, 1920, a picture of a new arrival for the Spokane airplane fleet was published in the paper. "Just arrived in Spokane from San Francisco," read the caption on the pictures, and it goes on to say:

> This is the new Curtiss Oriole plane, which reached Spokane last night from San Francisco. Danny Davidson, the pilot, is in the cockpit, while Norman Warsinski (left) and M. B. Martin, the owner, who made the trip, are standing at the side of the plane. Davidson was brought from Parkwater field to the city by Charles Sheeley in the light Overland shown in front of the plane.

The accompanying article goes on to say that the San Francisco to Spokane trip by plane took just 13 hours and 45 minutes, and the new 150 HP Curtiss Oriole was purchased by M. B. Martin, photographer. Incidentally, Martin was famous for photographs at this time, as were Foster Russell and Charles Libby and Sons. I have in my collection a number of old Spokane prints by all three of these gentlemen.

Again, a newspaper report dated May 3, 1920, reminds me of the other flying field I knew as a child. Headlines read:

> SPOKANE TO HAVE TWO FLYING FIELDS - Spokane, Wash. This city is to have two standard landing fields. The Russell-Symons Aviation Company's ground has been standardized for six months and has been in daily use throughout the winter. A four-machine hangar and repair shop is in operation. The Company operates a Curtiss Oriole, a JN-4, and a Standard Curtiss-engined machine. The city's Parkwater field [other one] is being placed in condition for landing under all conditions. This is the original flying field in Spokane and has been used by government flyers. The municipality has undertaken initial improvements at the field and is being utilized by the Spokane Aviation Company, just incorporated by W. T. Barnard, N. Barnard, D. Matthews and T. D. Matthews. William Durk, a student aviator, recently established an altitude record for Spokane by reaching 10,300 ft. level. A three passenger flying boat will be operated from Liberty Lake, ten miles east of Spokane, by the Russell-Symons company this summer.

On May 24, 1920, the paper carried the following article:

> SPOKANE AVIATION CO. HAS COMPLETE EQUIPMENT FOR AERIAL WORK - Spokane, Wash. With its four-plane hangar finished and the Parkwater field cleared of stones and leveled off, the Spokane Aviation Company has complete equipment for flying work. Commercial passenger carrying, a school of instruction and other lines of flying work will be done. The Parkwater field has been cleared up giving a fine four-way field with an east to west take off a mile and a half long.

CHAPTER 3 – THE POST WORLD WAR I BOOM

In this announcement, you can see how the two areas used by the pre-World War I pilots, which at that time were separated by stones, had been partially cleared to make one large landing area. This slow process of clearing apparently lasted for several years, because mention has been made to me of how Judge Stanley Webster had "allowed" the Spokane County chronic drunk and nonsupport prisoners to have "field exercise" by removing stones from the flying field area during 1922 and 1923. Also, Al Connick had mentioned that in the early days of the 116th Observation Squadron, 1924 and 1925, volunteers and flyers cleared rocks from the surface during any spare time they could find, with highly desirable results.

This race between Parkwater area activities on the north side of the valley and Foster Russell (Symons) on East Sprague had other aspects in history. In 1964 a person in New York City wrote to me while I was chairman of the Spokane Chamber of Commerce Aviation Committee asking if I would be interested in purchasing a couple of old drawings concerning an airport for Spokane, Washington. He had been cleaning out the old files of an engineering company and had noticed these two original drawings, and thought someone might be interested. I was. The material shows the layout of the facilities for the field at Parkwater in about 1919. The accuracy is not great, but the two separate areas south of the Spokane River at the Upriver Dam are shown complete with Bill Barnard's proposed hangar and the eternal "small boulders to be cleared." The same two fields were used by Deb Wylie in 1911.

The second drawing shows where the Foster Russell flying field was. Apparently Mr. Russell had planned on building his post-World War I flying field on the level ground near the present Spokane Community College Campus. This would be about one mile east of the Washington Water Power headquarters on Mission Avenue. The label "Foster Russell" marked on the roof of the hangar identifies this early plan, which of course was not built here, but at the intersection of what is now called Fancher Way (formerly Hardesty Road) and East Sprague Avenue (formerly the Appleway), just north of the railroad tracks.

It was here in about 1919-1920, that Tom Symons, a World War I-trained head pilot, and Foster Russell started their operation that was to compete with Parkwater. It continued for several years until Mr. Russell was killed in an airplane crash, and the company went out of business. Tom Symons became more interested in the field of broadcast radio and went on to a long and successful career in broadcasting.

Al Connick mentioned in one of his taped interviews how one of the planes at Foster Russell Airport was a Curtiss JN-4 that was painted blue and had the word "Hudson" painted on the side. This was an advertising gimmick for the Hudson automobile, which was sold by John Doran Co. "Jack" Doran was also a friend of Dad's, and we always had a Hudson or an Essex as a family auto during the years 1921 to 1929. His kids, Clyde, Dick, and Gen, went to school with us.

On June 4, 1920, the *Chronicle* reports:

> A factory for the construction of airplanes in Spokane is now pledged. Work is to begin within a few days for the building of a hangar at the Parkwater Aviation Field, according to an announcement made by R. C. Steeple, Treasurer of Northwest Aircraft Co. With the first successful flight of the Spokane-made plane, which took to the air for 22 minutes Friday at the Parkwater Field, the officers of the company have definitely decided to go on a plan of operation which will shortly result in the expenditure of several thousand dollars. We have been sort of hanging back until we demonstrated the value of our first Spokane-made machine, said Steeple. Now we are ready to go. A hangar to cost about $5,000 will be built at Parkwater right away and it is only a question of a short time when work will begin on our factory. There is a great demand for airplanes and there is no one to supply them. We could sell three or four planes right now if we had them built.

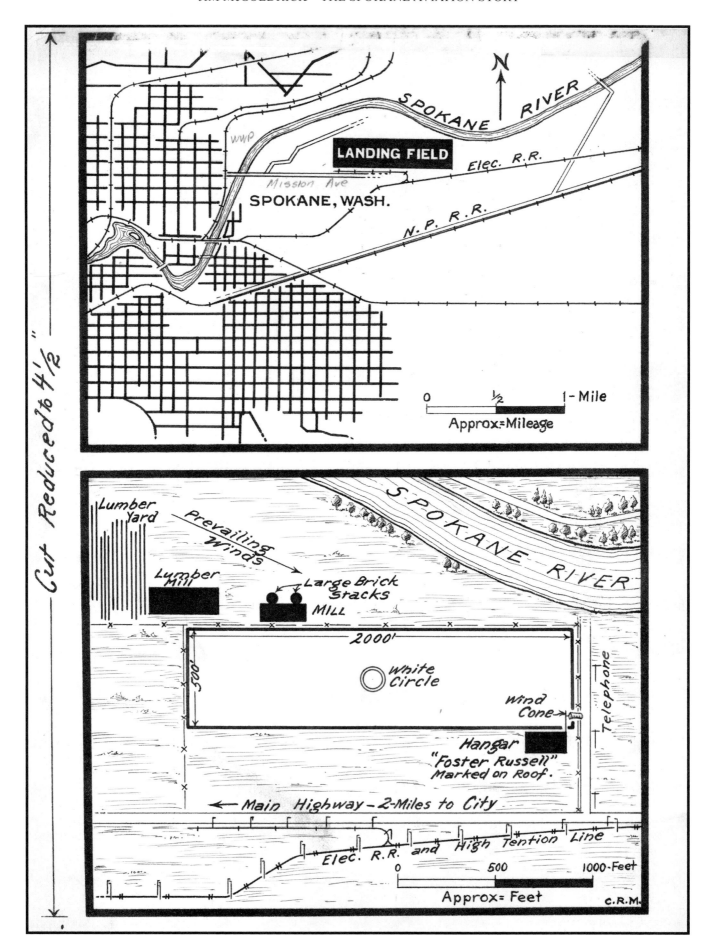

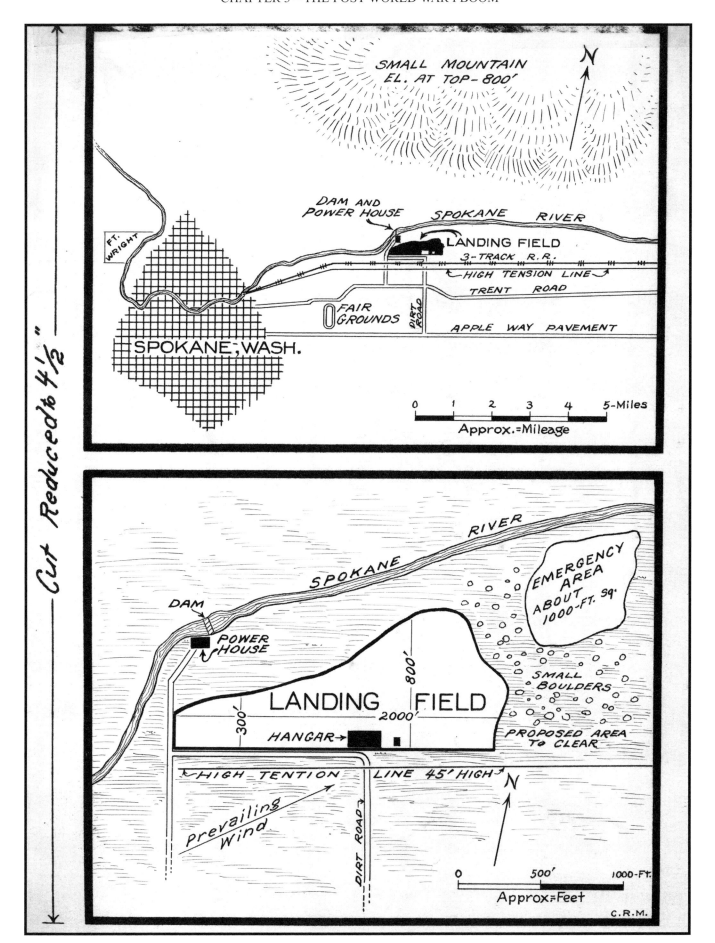

(Actually, it was at this time that the United States Government was trying to sell as surplus most of its large supply of Curtiss JN-4 training aircraft at prices which delayed the building of most postwar ships for several years.)

The *Spokane Daily Chronicle* continues to record the event:

> June 28, 1920 – A complete moving picture camera has been purchased by the United States Aircraft Corp., and will be used in connection with its aerial work, according to an announcement made today by C. H. Messer. "One of the first things I am going to do with the new camera is to take pictures while flying under the bridge at Lewiston, Idaho," Messer said. "Lieutenant Mamer, our chief pilot, flew under it last week. It should make an interesting film to show the approach to the bridge with the plane going at 80 or 90 miles an hour, then taking the bridge as it seemingly passes overhead. We will be able to take our own pictures of aerial exhibitions and events on the ground which can be taken from the air."

This is the first official mention I have of the United States Aircraft Corp, of Claude Messer, and of Nick Mamer, all to play an important part later in this story. Various quotations from the papers continue:

> June 30, 1920 – Patrons of the Coeur d'Alene Regatta on July 5, will be able to get big news of the day fresh off the presses of the Chronicle. Arrangements were completed today between C. H.. Messer, head of the United States Aircraft Corp., and H. L. McDuffie, circulation manager of the Chronicle, to take 1,200 papers to the regatta. Pilots Mamer and Fisher will probably pilot the planes. The papers will be taken from the *Chronicle* presses, hurried by automobile to the Parkwater field, packed aboard the two planes and taken to the Lake City in record time. Upon arriving there, the big bundles of paper will be dropped on the docks in view of thousands of people in the grandstand. Newsboys will be waiting. Forty minutes after the papers are printed, they will be in the hands of Coeur d'Alene readers.

> July 2, 1920 – A new Symons Bluebird which can be flown either from the land or the water, will be placed on Liberty Lake within the next ten days. A contract was closed with Lew Hurtig, in charge of the lake resort, giving Pilot Symons exclusive passenger-carrying rights from the beach. The plane is equipped with a 90 horsepower motor. It is a Standard J-l Model, and carries one passenger and a pilot. It is the only convertible airplane in the Northwest. This means that there will be a seaplane on the lake at every special occasion, Pilot Symons stated. It will be my headquarters for the summer. Many people prefer riding in a hydroplane to the regular airplane. The water equipment is already in the city and is being fitted to the plane. It requires only the changing of a few bolts to change the ship which flies from the land.

Incidentally, I remember Lew Hurtig from 1921 on. He was first the manager of Liberty Lake Park, owned by the railroad, and in its heyday one of the nicest. Later he bought it from the railroad and operated it until the 1930s when he sold it to Shay and Dimascus, who then turned it into the "Silver City" pavilion with a more modern, but less charming, character. The four Hurtig kids were very popular at Liberty Lake, and their father and mother did a great job of raising them.

From the *Chronicle* again, the story continues to unfold:

> A big first in air travel was scored for the Inland Empire at the Independence Day Celebration at Coeur d'Alene. A crowd estimated at 12,000 held its aggregate breath as a Curtiss Seagull arose from the surface of the lake. The plane, owned by Foster Russell, pioneer commercial air service operator, was the only one of its kind between the Pacific coast and Chicago, and the most costly aircraft here, being valued at $12,000. On its first Inland Empire flight the Seagull was piloted by Cleo Milton Filler of Pullman, a former Navy pilot. The novel craft was powered by an aluminum engine that weighed 417 pounds and produced 150 horsepower. It was capable of 100 MPH and on July 4, flew up the lake to Harrison in 20 minutes against the wind and back in 12. It can climb to 3,000 ft. in 10 minutes!

This was undoubtedly the "three passenger flying boat" referred to in the May 3, 1920, article previously mentioned. (I am not sure that it got to operate at Liberty Lake as planned. My uncle, my father and Tom

Symons all died before I could ask them about it. I would guess that the two-place Symons Bluebird with pontoons didn't work out too well, as a more powerful machine was needed on the water.

The *Coeur d'Alene Evening Press*, dated July 19, 1920, tells what finally happened to the Seagull:

> Seagull Crashes to Beach – Three Occupants are killed – Spectators at City Park see Pleasure Ride Converted into Dive to Death. At 2 o'clock yesterday afternoon the Seagull, piloted by Lieutenant Miller, and with George Erickson and Pete Savage as passengers, crashed in front of the City Park and the occupants of the plane were killed. The seaplane was flying over the park and had the appearance of making a landing. Thousands of people were watching the flight, and the majority are of the opinion that the power was cut off. The plane banked directly over the Regatta grandstands site and plunged downward, the bow striking first. Foster Russell states that it is impossible to ever know how the accident happened on account of the death of the pilot. He says that he was watching the ship and was surprised that Lieutenant Miller would attempt to make the bank with the ship traveling a slow speed. The loss, he estimates, to be about $7,000, which is covered by insurance (only the engine was salvaged). The Company to take over and operate the Seagull was to have met this morning to form the organization.

A more complete report in the *Spokesman-Review* dated July 19th echoes the same general story, but in addition mentions:

> William T. Barnard of Spokane Aviation Company left Parkwater Field, Spokane, with a S. R. staff reporter a few minutes after the accident, and arrived at the scene of the tragedy within an hour after its occurrence. The flight was made in 23 minutes and the return in 27 minutes.

One comment by a Mr. Scott, reported to be one of the prospective stockholders of the company, recounts:

> It was put in service on July 3, preparatory for flights during the regatta. On July 5th, it went out of order and needed repairing. On the 7th of July, while I was flying with Lt. Miller, while attempting to land, something went wrong and instead of landing in the water, we landed on the beach, the hull striking a log and damaging it to such an extent that it was laid up for several days. A few flights were made Saturday afternoon. Yesterday the plane was apparently in good running order. Twelve Coeur d'Alene men formed a corporation recently to operate seaplanes for pleasure flying at Coeur d'Alene. In addition to Mr. Scott, Major Glendeman of Coeur d'Alene was a heavy stockholder. The remainder were prominent businessmen here. A second plane of similar type was on a railroad car in the yards here awaiting unloading and setting up, as the company had plans to operate two planes during the summer.

My friend Bill Toth, who lived in Coeur d'Alene at the time, was playing baseball in the park and ran over to see what the excitement was about. Bill's comments tell how curious people on the beach crowded around the wreckage, picked up most of the small pieces and took them home as souvenirs, leaving only the large and too heavy items remaining. Thus ended the Seagull chapter in Spokane's aviation past.

About the same time, a clipping dated July 5th recounts that Nick Mamer flew to the Coeur d'Alene regatta, distributed 1,200 *Chronicles* and demonstrated the "upside down tailspin." Later, in August, he piloted the first commercial plane between Spokane and Wallace. Also in 1920, an announcement in the local newspaper brought to light the company which has been mentioned before that leads us to the famous Nick Mamer: "Mr. Spokane Aviation" of the roaring twenties and the Depression thirties.

> Lincoln-Standard Planes of U. S. Aircraft Corp. Spokane, Wash. -- Five Lincoln Standard Aeroplanes [note how they spelled airplanes in those days - British influence I think] purchased by the United States Aircraft Corporation have been delivered in Spokane and the work of setting them up is under way. C. H. Messer is manager of the corporation. Two of the planes have been used by the company for training purposes in the East, while three are new. The company has the agency in this district for the Lincoln Standard plane.

This brief statement is interesting for two reasons. General Wallace has told me that he remembers Claude Messer, as has Al Connick, and that he believed that Claude was associated with the Modern Auto Trac-

A crowd gathered following the crash of the Curtiss Seagull at Coeur d'Alene, July 7, 1920.

tor Co. Wallace should know because he was working in the Spokane automotive business before going into aviation during World War I. He points out how the young men were oriented to horses down on the farm until the war. Much mechanical progress was made then, and in the postwar era there was a shortage of skilled mechanics and operators for the new cars, trucks, farm machines and airplanes. Claude Messer managed such a school for training young men in these skills. The building they had at Parkwater was the same "Four-plane Hangar" built in 1920 by the Spokane Aviation Company (Bill Barnard & Associates). This we know. It burned in 1931. Did Bill Barnard's taking off with the cowling loose end the activities of Spokane Aviation and cause the sale of their investment to Modern Auto Tractor Co., which formed a flying-only division known as United States Aircraft Corp.? I think so, because Nick Mamer's daughter has mentioned that her father came to Spokane in 1920 to work for the "United States Aircraft Corp." The office, according to a photo of Nick Mamer, was at 1803 Third Avenue in Spokane. This connection brought Spokane's most famous aviator to our city for an all-too-short but outstanding career.

Another Spokane man, Harold Hahn, who was one of the sons of "Doc" Rudolph Hahn, well-known Spokane racing car owner, was sent to Minnesota in 1920 to buy war surplus equipment for Modern Auto Tractor Company. This included several airplanes and it is believed that Nick Mamer came to Spokane as a result of the purchase. Harold Hahn was associated with the aircraft repair business at Felts Field for many years, mostly with Wallace Aeromotive.

Nicholas Bernard Mamer – who was he? A thumbnail sketch is necessary here to set the stage for his many Spokane aviation accomplishments. Nick was born in Hastings, Minnesota, on January 28, 1898. As a young man he was well known to visitors of the various county fairs where he performed many daring feats, in motorcycle races and parachute jumps, according to his daughter, Mrs. Leo Lee of Seattle. She states that he ran away from home when he was 16 and later joined the Army, although he had some flying experience before this time. An early newspaper clipping she has tells that Nick was "Minnesota's first recruit in Army aviation."

The wreckage of the Curtiss Seagull.

According to an article in the *Seattle Post Intelligencer* dated Sunday, January 26, 1964, concerning the flight of the *Spokane Sun-God* and Nick Mamer and Art Walker, he won his wings and lieutenant's bars at Kelly Field, Texas, and served with the American Expeditionary Forces in France during World War I. His commanding officer wrote afterwards:

> It is my pleasure to certify that Lt. N. B. Mamer was attached to the 187th Aero Squadron, A.E.F. [American Expeditionary Force] on active duty as pursuit pilot from July 14, 1918 to December 1, 1918. He contributed to the valor of the squadron by being awarded the French Croix de Guerre with Palms, in addition to three citations. Lieutenant Mamer is officially credited with the destruction of three enemy planes. His plane was shot down in flames in combat with three enemy Fokker planes near Dun sur Meuse, France, November 2, 1918, during the Argonne battle. By skillful judgment and superb cool-headedness he managed his plane in such a way as to protect himself, during the descent, from the flames. The plane being demolished upon landing, his presence of mind enabled him to extricate himself from the wreckage, thereby saving his life and escaping with minor injuries.

At this point there is a divergence of opinion regarding Nick's exact wartime duty. In 1939, at the dedication ceremony of the Mamer memorial clock at Felts Field, the *Spokane Daily Chronicle* of Tuesday, May 30th tells of a file of newspaper clippings at the W.F.A. (Western Front Association) office in Spokane. These state that he "learned to fly at 18 at the Curtiss School of Aviation in San Diego. He served in the World War in the Seventh Aero Squadron, first combat squad, Canal Zone."

I am not sure which report is exactly correct, but having known him slightly during his Spokane years, I can understand that, with his extreme modesty and quiet way, he could have been quite a hero during the war without saying much about it! Hillford Wallace states that it was the understanding of the pilots in the 116th that he was on duty in the Canal Zone. In either case, Nick Mamer was responsible for more aviation firsts being credited to Spokane than any other person. He was a trusted, respected and admired leader of Spokane commercial aviation in those trying early days.

Some of those activities are described in the text that follows, but to show how he rated in our family, I recall March 18, 1928. On this day, to celebrate my Grandmother Lawson's 70th birthday, Grandma, Dad,

A display at the Spokane Interstate Fair in 1920 by the Modern Automobile & Tractor School, featuring their aviation division known as the United States Aircraft Corp. The school had a number of students enrolled in the auto and tractor courses at its Spokane headquarters at West 1803 Third Avenue. The pilot training was at the hangar at Parkwater. The company also had branches at Seattle and St. Paul.

Mom, sister Betty and I went for a ride with Nick in the old Buhl Airsedan. Even at that time, he had the reputation for being the safest pilot in Spokane (maybe even the world), and we trusted him completely. The plane had a Wright 220 horsepower J-5 engine with the pilot up front with a single stick and a cabin for four amidships. Several weeks later Dad and I went with Nick in the Waco 10 with a Curtiss OX-5 and experienced our first loop and other routine acrobatics. When Dad and his lumbering associates had a meeting in Bend, Oregon, or some hard to get place, they would charter Nick and his plane to safely take them there and back – but these memories are getting ahead of the story.

Nick Mamer, Mamer Flying Service, in front of airplane, March 6, 1929. *(Courtesy MAC, Libby photo L87-1.38739-29)*

Nick Mamer and companions flew two Lincoln-Standard planes from St. Paul in 1920, the first of a fleet of five owned by the Modern Automobile & Tractor School, whose flying department was to be known as the United States Aircraft Corp. The sign painted on the fuselage urges all to "Learn a Trade." The six-cylinder in-line engines are probably Hall Scott water-cooled, popular at that time. Note the vertical radiator.

Nick Mamer, right, and friend in 1923. The plane is thought to be a Hisso Lincoln-Standard.

Mamer Air Transport's Ryan B-1 in 1928. It was on Spokane-Portland run and nicknamed the "Columbia Gorge Express" because it flew through the Gorge, under the weather!

The Mamer Flying Service's two hangars at the west end in 1929, on the present site of Spokane Community College aviation facility.

CHAPTER 3 – THE POST WORLD WAR I BOOM

The following Associated Press release dated June 1, 1923 reported the statistics concerning flying safety at this time and gives a good idea how things were then throughout the United States:

ITINERANT FLYERS SUFFER HEAVY TOLL

New York, June 1, -- (Associated Press)-- The causes for the airplane accidents of 1922, and recommendations for the reduction of future accidents to a minimum, are found in the annual report of the Aeronautical Chamber of Commerce of America to the Secretary of Commerce. The chamber says the government must provide air law and exercise jurisdiction over all civil flying if casualties are to be reduced. The report indicates that most of the 1922 accidents were due to the itinerant pilot who has no fixed base, is unlicensed and unregulated by law, and therefore has no presumptive responsibility. Of approximately 1,200 civilian airplanes in operation in the United States in 1922, says the report, between 550 and 600 were owned among 130 established operators, that is, individuals and organizations with fixed bases and conservative business policies: an equal number were distributed among itinerant pilots who have no particular system and depend for a living upon stunting, barnstorming tours, and extra hazardous assignments.

In 1922 there were 122 accidents among the itinerant pilots, or gypsies, and only 12 among the fixed base operators. These accidents resulted in 62 fatalities among the gypsies and only seven among the fixed base operators. One hundred persons were injured through accidents with so-called gypsy planes and only seven were hurt in planes operated from fixed bases.

ESTABLISHED OPERATORS EFFICIENT

The 130 established operators, having definite financial responsibility, fields, repair shops in a majority of cases, and a system of inspection for their craft, demonstrated a degree of dependability by older and officially regulated mediums of transportation. They incurred only 12 accidents in 1922 as against 24 accidents in 1921. And many of these could have been avoided had there been in effect federal laws licensing operators.

In startling contrast is the record of the gypsies. They have consistently replaced their damaged equipment with the obsolete surplus from government stores remaining from war production and available at prices so cheap that youths with often a few hundred dollars may and invariably do, acquire airplanes which they alter to accommodate one or two paying passengers. The passengers are led to ride in these machines through ignorance of safety factors controlling flight, and the public generally seems to accept all aircraft as airworthy, not pausing to reflect that here is the only vehicle of importance which the operators are not compelled by law to make and operate in a manner calculated to safeguard the public.

From 500 to 600 of these gypsy craft have wandered from town to town for at least two years. According to the most complete accounts obtainable, in 1921 there were 114 accidents involving itinerant fliers. In 1922 there were 126 accidents, an increase of twelve. In 1921 the accidents resulted in 49 fatalities and 89 persons injured; in 1922, 62 fatalities and 100 persons injured, an increase of 13 deaths, or more than 26 percent, and 11 injured, or more than 12 percent.

Among the gypsy fliers, 37 accidents were due to lack of inspection of their equipment. Government licensing and other regulations would have prevented this. Poor piloting caused 46 accidents, stunting caused 39 accidents, also preventable by federal regulations, 11 were caused by carelessness on fields and 17 were from unknown causes, 14 to lack of landing fields, one to lack of weather data, nine to lack of route data., in which the pilots became lost and were driven off their course.

In other words, 30 percent of the accidents were among itinerants. The vast majority of these accidents were caused by stunting, and 29 percent to faulty inspection of aircraft. This seems to afford sufficient evidence that federal regulations, providing primarily for the licensing of pilots as to competency, the prohibition of dangerous flying, and for the certification of equipment as to airworthiness, will operate to correct abuses in aviation and make flying safer.

Thus the stage was set for the coming of government regulation that appeared a few years later in the form of the Department of Commerce, Civil Aeronautics Authority, which later became the Federal Aviation Agency.

Also in 1923, Nick Mamer was said to have the first contract with the U.S. Forest Service for patrolling the Inland Empire forests during the fire season, but details on this 1923 date are lacking and it may have been confused with his 1925 contract described later.

Jim Ford, longtime active manager of the Spokane Chamber of Commerce, mentioned in a brief historical paper in 1950 how, in 1920 Spokane had decided that it must have a municipal landing field. There were no such things as "airports" at that time. As a result, the city commissioners and the park board set aside what is now known as Felts Field (originally called Parkwater), which at that time was a part of the city park area, so Spokane could have an air landing field. The next thing was to get some flying on the field, so the Chamber hurried and scurried and hustled to find users for our new field.

In 1926 the Department of Commerce officially recognized Spokane's flying field and designated it an airport. Spokane had one of the first airports in the West, in fact one of the first officially recognized airports in the United States.

OX-5 Standard (90 horsepower) at Parkwater Field, 1923.

Hisso Standard (180 horsepower Wright), 1926.

Airplane propellers displayed in front of Modern Automobile & Tractor School, West 1803 Third Avenue, 1920. *(Courtesy Mac, Libby photo L87-1.18250-20)*

The United States Aircraft Corporation hangar at Parkwater in 1920. The small sign on the right end of the wall is that of the Spokane Aviation Company, which built the hangar the previous year and sold to the new owners. It advises: "Planes fly from this field – Flights daily – Trips anywhere. Pilots Dave Matthews, Wm. Barnard, N. Barnard." The two Lincoln-Standard planes flown from St. Paul are in front, while one of the three planes being assembled is in the open end of the hangar. Later the building was used for storage by the 116th Observation Squadron, then burned in a gasoline fire.

TYPE OF PLANE TO BE BUILT IN SPOKANE

This English type airplane is to be manufactured in Spokane according to plans announced today by the United States Aircraft Co. The plane is the English Avro Avian, for which United States manufacturing rights have been secured by the Spokane concern. It is a two-seated machine with an 80-horsepower engine that develops a cruising speed of from 85 to 90 miles an hour and a maximum speed of 105 miles an hour. Six of these planes will be constructed here before spring, according to officials of the new concern.

AIRPLANE FACTORY WILL OPEN IN CITY

Spokane Men Incorporate for $100,000—Engine and Parts Factory Coming.

An airplane construction company, with American manufacturing rights for a popular English plane, has been established in Spokane and production will be started this spring.

This announcement was made

A article announcing an airplane manufacturing plant to be opened in Spokane stated the following: "The name of the company is the United States Aircraft Corporation. When the planes are completed they will be priced from $1,800 to 2,000. The engines for the planes will be 80-horsepower and will be built by the Washington Machinery and Supply Company. The company plans to build 25 planes the first year and increase to 50 the following year. Each plane will be equipped with duo controls and be able to fly a maximum of 105 miles an hour."

A happy group in a new 1927 Buick Roadster with rumble seat in front of a DH-4 at Parkwater.

A downtown Spokane car and plane showroom in 1929.

Major John T. "Jack" Fancher, beloved first commander of the Washington Air National Guard.

Our National Guard Squadron

Officers of the 116th Observation Squadron WNG in 1925. Front row: Felts, Sherman, Hicks; Henry; Peters; Fancher; Maj. Emmons, who was inspecting the squadron; Easterbrook; Bill Williams, the federal instructor; ? ... ? ... Bob Owen. Second row: Tom Symons, Neely; Wallace; ?m ... ? ; Wadsworth.

Nineteen twenty-four was another milestone in Spokane aviation history. A small group of Spokane businessmen, including R. I. Rutter and William H. Cowles Sr., both progressive backers of aviation, had raised about $12,000 to prove to Governor Roland Hartley that Spokane was behind a move to form a National Guard Squadron here. The money was to be used to put down concrete slabs for the floor of two World War I surplus airplane hangars, which had been prefabricated to be sent overseas, but were then declared surplus at the conclusion of the war. With the leadership of Major John T. "Jack" Fancher from Medical Lake, who had an "envious record as an officer in France with the air forces," the governor and Adjutant General Maurice Thompson granted the request and 116th Aviation Squadron was organized. The first summer, 1924, saw the unloading from the railroad cars of the hangars, their erection on the slabs and the general organization of the unit. Also the removal of more rocks!

It was in March 1924 that our good family friend Lawrence Sherman came to Spokane after he had graduated from Kelly Field in Texas. "Sherm" said his first job offer was to fly liquor down from Canada at night to a "small field opposite Felts" in a Hisso Standard. He declined, instead joining the new National Guard Squadron.

A clipping from the St. Maries, Idaho, *Gazette Record* dated September 18, 1924, reports: "Lt. Nick Mamer, with his airplane, was a St. Maries visitor Saturday and Sunday and did a good business taking up passengers for short flights. A feature of the visit was a parachute jump from the machine at an elevation of 1500 feet, making a successful landing near the air field."

By the spring of 1925, the 116th had the original 13 officers, plus several new ones and a good number of young enlisted men all interested in aviation-related activities, and anxious to do their "week end soldiering" as reservists. Major Fancher was the commanding officer, while captains Lawrence Albert, Robert Owen, Lawrence Sherman and Claude Owen out-ranked lieutenants Hillford R. Wallace, Sam Hicks, Edward Axberg, Buell Felts, Harold Neely, William Williams, Tom Symons and Ed Bigelow. Soon after, Lt. Jack Allenberg, Einar Malstrom, Byron Cooper, Dick Gleason, Jack Rose and Ray Shrock were aboard, according to General Wallace in 1974. A little later Elsworth French became public information officer and Dwight Smith a flying officer. Others followed.

During the two weeks encampment of the 116th in June 1925, the outfit was being whipped into military readiness and the press was active in telling the story to the public. At this time the National Guard flying field at Parkwater was referred to as "Camp Earl Hoisington" field. I am not sure where this name came from, but feel it might have more to do with the annual training camp area than the airport. (This may have been like the "Geiger Field" military portion of "Spokane International Airport" in later years.) In any event, the name disappeared from use and apparently gave way to the shorter name "SPOKANE AIR PORT," which was painted on the roof of the west main hangar (a very long roof would have been needed to paint the former).

An interesting sidelight concerns Lt. Jack Rose. According to my longtime friend, Carl Partlow, who also was a friend of Jack's family, he changed his name from "Eddie" Le Beau to the more easily pronounced Jack Rose. There was some kind of joke about Jack taking off and rising into the sky – hence Jack rose!

The *Spokesman Review* of June 18, 1925, had a picture of Major John Fancher under the heading of HEADS AVIATION UNIT:

> With an envious record in the war as an officer in France with the air force, Major John Fancher, who is shown above, has won his majority in the national guard air unit and is in command of the 116th aviation squadron now in training at Camp Earl Hoisington field at Parkwater. Major Fancher has an organization that has been extolled by both Governor Hartley and Adjutant General Maurice Thompson, both of whom have been taken on rides above the city.

Three days later the paper, in covering the news of the two weeks encampment, shows a picture of several planes "on the line" and state:

> Hoisington field of the 161st observation squadron, national guard, all dressed up for an inspection of the executive committee of the Chamber of Commerce, whose members were guests of the Aviation unit last week. Two of the D. H. planes are seen in the foreground, and the rows of tents for the personnel can be seen in the rear. Army officers inspecting the field have declared it in fine shape and the squadron one of the best.

This sounds quite believable because Spokane was the third national guard aerial squadron formed in the U.S. The second to form was Minnesota. Note that the squadron was referred to as the 161st "Observation" Squadron rather than the 116th "Aviation" Squadron. This is probably because the 161st Infantry (41st Division) was based at Fort Wright and then the Armory and initially was instrumental in forming the aviation group. Later the squadron had a photo section.

Clippings continue to tell the story:

> GUARD AVIATOR INJURED IN FALL – Sgt. Ed Craney Hurt When Pole He is on Topples Over at Parkwater. The training of national guard aviators at Camp Earl Hoisington field at Parkwater was marred yesterday by a serious injury of Sergeant Craney of the 116th Aviation Squadron. The Sergeant, who suffered severe bruises and probably internal injuries, was injured in a fall, but not from an airplane. He was aiding in the raising of a 30 ft. pole to be used in radio work on the field and was at the top to which he had strapped himself. It fell after it had been raised upright, hurling him to the ground. He was stunned by the force of the blow and it was first feared killed.

This is interesting to me because Ed Craney became chief engineer for Tom Symons's radio station KFPY and his partner in several other radio stations in the Northwest. He was the first owner of Spokane's Channel 4 television station and then CH-6 in Butte. I remember when he and Tom Symons and Lawrence Sherman had an Austin (British small car) agency in the Symons Building during the late 1920s. During a Christmas afternoon visit to my family, Lawrence Sherman drove the little Austin (complete with wife and daughter) up the sidewalk and parked it at the front porch.

Other information says:

> Major General Thompson, commander of the National Guard forces of the State, made an official inspection of the field yesterday and took an air ride with Major Fancher, Commandant. He expressed pleasure at the advancement of the field and of the flyers and troops being trained there. The flyers and troops are going through their regular drill every day with pilots taking different members of the troop on rides each day and putting them through all the stunts as passengers.

Also about the same time, another headline states: "Test is Success – Army Airmen 2000 Feet Up Chat with Mates on Ground." (This was the test Ed Craney was setting equipment up for the previous week.)

The 1925 article goes on to say:

> Seated in the hangar at Spokane Flying field Tuesday afternoon, Lieutenant H. R. Neely heard plainly a voice from the clouds. The voice was that of Second Lieutenant L. B. Graham, radio expert, who at the time was flying some 2000 feet above the ground with Pilot Nick Mamer. From now until the end of the encampment, Saturday night, the men are to be instructed in the use of the radio and Wednesday artillery missions are to be used. In warfare the practice is known as "puff" communications. Smoke bombs, fired by artillery, are easily discernible to the pilot and observer, who mark where the shell lights and then signal range corrections to those on the ground. The Lincoln plane, carrying the radio equipment is equipped with a generator, functioning on a tiny propeller. A receiving set in the observers seat is fastened securely into place and forms the medium by which the man in the seat may carry on a conversation with those below him or in another plane.

If all this seems rather elementary, remember, very few people in 1925 owned a radio set because it was just starting to become a household device.

The *Spokesman Review,* June 20, 1925, has a picture of two pilots standing in front of a JN-6 in the usual flying togs, silk scarf, leather helmet, goggles, leather jacket, etc. The article stated:

> Here are two of the men who are important factors in the success of the National Guard Aviation unit at Parkwater field. Major John Fancher in command, is on the left, Lieutenant Nick Mamer, a veteran pilot of Spokane, is standing next to

him. They gave a thrilling exhibition of airmanship last week before members of the military affairs committee of the Chamber of Commerce. They were photographed upon coming down out of the clouds.

It would seem appropriate here to try to identify the status of Lt. Nick Mamer during these times. He was not listed as one of the "charter" officers of the 116th National Guard Observation Squadron; in fact there is some indication that he was not a regular member of the squadron. Possibly, as an Army Air Corps reservist and professional pilot of exceptional skill and experience, he was hired at first to help Major Jack Fancher instruct and train the new and relatively green "weekend" pilots. He thus apparently had all the privileges of an officer in the Guard, but few, if any, of the compulsory duties. Nick never rose above the rank of lieutenant in the military, probably because he did not choose to do so. After all, he was busy at first with his barnstorming and then with his commercial flying activities and contracts. He headed the Mamer Flying Service (and Flying School) and later the Mamer Air Transport.

The new Washington National Guard Squadron always had full-time personnel from the Army. Since most of the membership consisted of volunteers who drilled about once a week, the organization was led and supervised by a small group of professionals furnished by the Army.

Where originally Nick Mamer may have been hired to help in this important duty, he soon gave way to military career men like Major Haynes, Major Breen and finally Major Wallace (after he had put in several years active duty at the Presidio).

Also in this category was Master Sgt. John Simpson who played an important role in whipping the boys into shape during the 16 years before World War II. After the war, he retired from the military and worked with Harold Hahn at Wallace Aeromotive at Felts Field.

Towards the end of the training encampment, press reports had so intrigued the citizens that many of them came out to the airport to see for themselves just what it was like. One Sunday the boys were having a "rest day" from the normally strenuous routine. The following newspaper report tells how it was many years ago:

AVIATION FIELD DRAWS SCORES

Guards Keep Back Enthusiastic Admirers of Flying Machines at Hoisington Field.
YOUNG WOMAN THRILLED
Harrington Postmaster, Wife and Son Go Up – Learn Use of Bag at End of Pole

Earl Hoisington field at Parkwater, home of the national guard flying unit now on encampment there, drew hundreds of sightseers and friends and relatives of the troopers yesterday afternoon. As many as 150 automobiles were parked, and while Lieutenant Nick Mamer flew and circled with passengers, in a corner of the field a baseball game raged while in the shade of a building a trooper with a Hawaiian guitar drew his share of the crowd.

"What's that thing for?" Everybody asks some one in authority, referring to a bag attached to a pole and which whirls and puffs out in the breeze on top of one of the airdromes. The bag is to show the direction of the wind so the flyers will know which way to "take off" from the field, it was explained. They always take off from the ground against the wind, as there is less danger of accident.

But while there was interest in the baseball game between the aviation unit and a Hillyard team, and while there were many charmed by the guitar player's melodies, Lieutenant Nick Mamer and his big plane were the feature of the afternoon. When Mamer, who is considered one of the best aviators here, sauntered to his plane, and with the aid of a sergeant started it going, there was an eager rush toward it and guards had to keep the crowd back.

The first encampment at Camp Earl Hoisington at Parkwater in June 1925.

September 14, 1925, with the full squadron on the "line." On the left is the small building that was constructed by Bill Barnard & Associates in 1920.

JN-6 trainers and DH-4s were the planes of the squadron in 1925-26.

Art Stimson takes a picture of a DH-4 on take-off in 1925.

Squadrons also needed trucks . . .

. . . and hangars . . .

. . . and motor cars and motorcycles . . .

. . . and officers . . .

. . . and men . . .

YOUNG WOMEN MAKE AIR TOUR

Residents of the Breslin apartments are proud of the view from the roof garden of their building, but Mrs. Thelma Leighton and Miss Julia Jayne, who live there, now agree it doesn't amount to so much. The reason for their new decision was a tour above the city yesterday on which they were conducted by Nick Mamer. It was the first ride for both young women and a little of the war spirit was given it by the fact that Miss Jayne wore the helmet worn by Major Fancher, commandant of the field, during his service in France. Mamer, circling back to the field, stunted to the ground, and when they landed they agreed it was the greatest thrill of their lives.

HARRINGTON POSTMASTER GOES UP

Then A. J. Grant, Postmaster at Harrington, and Mrs. Grant went up for a ride, and their son followed them. Mr. and Mrs. Grant are the parents of Mrs. Langley, whose husband is flight surgeon at the field. And following them were a number more. The day was hot at the field and the flying weather was good. First Sergeant McDermott, former house detective at the Davenport, was kept busy at the company canteen near the field grounds serving pop and ice-cream. Captain Albert tried to keep cool in the shade of a building, not permitting the ball game, the guitar music or the flying to interfere in his quest for shade.

As a result of this great display of interest by the public in the activities of the new squadron, Major Fancher decided it would be appropriate to put on a full blown air circus for the citizens later in the year. This is why the September 20th event was developed, description of which follows chronologically later in the text.

A week after the encampment was over, on June 29, 1925, the *Spokane Chronicle* stated:

MAMER NAMED FOREST PATROL FLYING OFFICER

Lieutenant Nick B. Mamer of Spokane today received appointment as forest fire patrol pilot for Eastern Washington, Northern Idaho and Western Montana He will leave Spokane tomorrow night for Rockwell field, San Diego, to get his Liberty-motored De Haviland airplane, which will be used on the patrol. A second pilot will be named soon to fly a similar ship over the same area. The National Guard hangars in Spokane will be the field base for Mamer's forest patrol airplanes, according to official instructions. That will make Spokane headquarters for the entire district in fire patrol work for the area. Pilot Mamer's standing as one of the most capable, and experienced, flyers in the west won him this opportunity. It is considered an important task inasmuch as the greater part of the flying is over rugged country where it require: great skill to make safe landings in the event of motor trouble. The instructions indicate that the patrol work will be begun as soon as the plane reaches Spokane. Pilot Mamer said, "That should be some time next week. The trip north, with favorable conditions should take but two or three days." Pilot Mamer said, "his orders carry no intimation as to when the second plane and pilot will be on the job."

General Wallace explained to me in 1978 that the two DH-4 aircraft were loaned to the U.S. Forest Service by the Army Air Corps. The Forest Service hired Nick and another pilot to fly the patrol to determine if this activity would be helpful in controlling the seasonal forest fires. Apparently it proved valuable because it continued for years as a regular cog in the machinery to preserve our forest resources.

In early September there appeared in the paper a picture of nine fearless aviators lined up, complete with goggles. The caption read:

National Guard Aviators Hop Off in Planes for Coast

Commanded by Major Jack Fancher, five national guard airplanes hopped off from municipal field yesterday en route to Vancouver, Wash., where they will take part in the dedication of Parson Field. Later this week they will return to Spokane to take part in the gigantic air circus to be held Saturday and Sunday. Left to right, those in the picture are: Lt. Harold Neely, Major Fancher, Major James Sabiston, Lt. Tom Symons, Sgt. Paul Sager, Pvt. Swineheart, Lt. Al Axberg, Lt. George Henry and Master Sgt. Charles Holter.

Pictures of Jack Rose's wrecked Stearman (with Wright J-5) resulting from a power failure while on a forest patrol mission over rugged terrain in the 1930s. Note: The engine was being taken apart so that it could be carried out, as there were no roads near the crash site.

An Army Fokker tri-motor visited the 116th in 1925.

The Pvt. Swineheart mentioned is Dr. Paul Swineheart of Spokane, who was an active optometrist on Riverside Avenue for many years. He has mentioned this particular trip on several recorded sessions of the "Old Time Pilots" group organized by Bill Toth.

After Paul had joined the squadron in 1925 as a private and on this trip was acting as an observer for his friend Lt. George Henry in a JN-6 Jenny (180 HP Hisso), they encountered a strong headwind. As a result, they were forced to land at Lind and then Kennewick. Their next stop for fuel was to be Goldendale. By this time George was asleep in the front cockpit and Paul was flying. All of a sudden the main tank went dry and in switching to the reserve tank, the engine quit entirely and they made a forced landing in a farm field on a bluff just overlooking the Columbia River. Since the Jenny didn't have any brakes, they narrowly missed rolling over the rim of the field into the gully below. They landed by a small farmhouse. The farmer was delighted to meet his first flying men. They put some tractor fuel in the plane, pulled it back up the hill with a team of horses, killed a chicken and fixed biscuits, and spent the evening at dinner talking with their host. The next morning they were able to take off and continue to Vancouver.

After the exercises at Pearson Field, the squadron of four Jennys and a DH-4 headed back to Spokane via the Pendleton Rodeo where they shook a few hands and displayed the friendship of Spokane. The next day Lt. Henry landed in a field near Pullman and Paul grabbed his suitcase and walked to Washington State College to begin his school year, leaving the pilot to return to Spokane alone. Paul brags he was one of the first college students to be flown to class in an airplane.

The following Sunday, September 20, 1925, a "Gigantic Air Circus" was held at Parkwater, according to Al Connick, "to publicize Liberty Bonds." Airplanes from San Francisco and Minneapolis, as well as local pilots, were heavily involved. During the show a wet blanket was placed on the affair when the Ministerial Association was partially successful in their attempt to stop the activities, which they were against because they were on Sunday. According to Connick, the ministers wired Governor Roland Hartley who sent down an order that "all State owned aircraft were to remain on the ground." Lt. Pring, Lt. Priestley, Lt. Nick Mamer had just completed the DH-4 race. The De Haviland DH-4s had big 400 I-IF Liberty engines and were the most powerful and best planes at the time. Because stunt pilots could climb out and hang on the prop, these planes were a great favorite with them. The pilots argued that many of the aircraft were not state owned and so the De Havilands were used to continue the show program.

At this point a tragedy occurred when Lt. Priestley and Pvt. Avey went aloft in a 180 HP JN-6 aircraft for a balloon busting contest. Having just gotten out of the more powerful plane, Lt. Priestley stalled the low performance Jenny and spun into the ground from a low altitude. The plane landed in a pit on the west margin of the field near the waterworks building. Al Connick was standing a few hundred feet away, as was newly married Dwight Smith, and they rushed over to find both airmen, members of the 116th Observation Squadron, had been killed.

On this same day, I was standing in the road that is now called Fancher Way at a point halfway between Parkwater and the Foster Russell Airport. I can still see the black smoke coming up from the crash and had to wait till the following morning newspaper to read of the details. My family had driven out to see the show after Sunday 1:30 p.m. dinner and, as a result, we were unable to get very close to the airfield due to the large crowd in attendance. This accident was the first fatality of the Parkwater Field, which is now known as Felts Field, and was my first observed fatality.

The gathering at the September 1925 Air Circus at the Spokane Airport. *(National Guard photo)*

A more complete and accurate report is contained in a clipping dated September 21, 1925, from the Seattle *Morning Star:*

PLANE CRASH IS FATAL TO TWO SPOKANE MEN Army Flyers Killed When machine Falls 400 feet 30,000 SEE ACCIDENT Aircraft Plunges Into Nose Dive Over Field. "SPOKANE, Sept. 21 – Two Spokane army flyers were killed when their plane crashed 400 feet to the ground in an air circus staged here yesterday afternoon. 1st Lieut. Schuyler Priestley, 30, reserve pilot, was driving the plane, a Curtiss SJN-6-H, with Pvt. John A. Avey, Jr., 20, national guardsman, as observer. Thirty thousand persons witnessed the tragic accident which occurred above Earl Hoisington field while 23 planes were maneuvering in the air. The other planes continued their flights in a vain effort to attract attention from the plane fall. The plane dropped into a nose dive while circling. Avey was killed instantly. Priestley died as he was being lifted into an ambulance. Regular army flyers were not permitted to fly yesterday after the Spokane Ministerial Association wired a protest against the Sunday flying circus. Lieutenant Priestley had won a speed race shortly before the fatal crash. He had been driving a DeHaviland machine for the big exhibition flight.

The following letter dated December 27, 1980 from my father's and my old friend Colonel Lawrence Sherman gives a firsthand account of the way he remembers the day:

Dear Jim:

I've really enjoyed your draft of Spokane's aviation history, particularly the period from 1911 to the time I arrived in Spokane in 1924. You have done some great research of this early period and I never before knew there was this much flying activity as far back as 1911. This is fascinating stuff. The only area I might clarify concerns the Air Circus - I was involved a great deal in that and so was your Dad. I don't think Al Connick was familiar with some of the inside

CHAPTER 4 – OUR NATIONAL GUARD SQUADRON

details of this situation. The cause of all the trouble was the Rev. Louis Magin of the Methodist Church. Without consulting the other members of the Ministerial Association – or anyone else that I know of – he sent a wire to Gov. Hartley and also to the War Department stating that the Sabbath abiding people of Spokane objected strongly to this 'Circus' being held on the Sabbath day although the Guard Squadron held their weekly drills and flying missions every Sunday morning to which there had never been any objection. Probably the word CIRCUS set him off – we probably should have called it an Air Show. Present at the field was a squadron of DH's from Crissy Field, Frisco, a Reserve squadron of Jennies from Portland and the same from Seattle plus the Spokane squadron of Jennies.

Hartley had jurisdiction only over the Spokane Squadron and took no action; the War Department however wired back that no regular army aircraft would participate which left the three forest patrol DH's and the Spokane, Portland and Seattle jenny squadrons to put on the show. This 'grounding' by the War Department came Saturday afternoon. A committee went out to visit Rev. Magin to try to get him to call off the ban but he refused, then the committee which I think included your Dad, Vic Desert and others were up most of the night trying to call influential people in Washington while a few of the Squadron officers including myself were up most of the night revising the flying program for the next day, which also meant that we would have to put on most of the show. The next day I never flew so many different kinds of missions in my life

The three forestry DH's, although Army aircraft were on loan to the Dept. of Agriculture and consequently did not come under the War Department grounding, so flew their race. The three pilots then were Nick Mamer, Ragnar Freng and Priestly who flew the forestry contract for $400 per month of a three months contract. Priestly incidentally was a classmate of mine at Kelly Field, lived in Portland and was a member of the Reserve Squadron there.

At the time of his crash we were scheduled for a balloon busting contest. I was the entry for the Spokane Squadron, Priestly for the Portland Squadron – I don't remember the name of the Seattle entry. I was first and Priestly was floating around the edges at reduced throttle waiting for me to finish. As you know a Jenny whips off into a spin at anywhere near a stall speed and that's what happened – they don't float like a DH.

The aftermath of this was rough. A number of downtown stores pasted the newspaper accounts in the window underlining Fancher's statement 'that these boys were sacrificed on the altar of religious bigotry' and the underlining in red ran out to the margin to the word 'murder' which lost Magin a large section of his congregation and he finally asked for a transfer. I have gone into some detail on this so you will have the whole story – use whatever you want any way you want.

An interesting footnote on Freng: He later became an airline pilot I think with United and finally retired while still whole. He is mentioned in one of McCann's books and while still flying on a stopover in Miami got caught in one of their bad hurricanes. Apparently he got involved in a lot of rescue work – I've forgotten the details – and received a lot of national publicity and some award or other.

You might explore some more of the 116th's antics – there were some screwy as well as interesting experiences although I'm not sure they really fit a history. After the Lindbergh flight every town in Washington and Idaho had to have an airfield and the Squadron was very popular – we had to put on a show at every one plus Apple Blossom Festivals plus even a mule show. . . . Please give my regards to all the 'older' QBs – and my best to all of you for the New Year. Sincerely, Sherm

November 15, *Spokane Chronicle*:

Two hundred people stood with bared heads in the rain yesterday to pay tribute to the memory of John Avey, private in the national guard, who was killed in an airplane crash during the air circus last September. The occasion was the unveiling of his monument, erected by the women's auxiliary to the national guard, which had charge of the services yesterday. A firing squad, made up of members of Avey's company, sent three volleys across the grave, and a bugler from Fort Wright sounded taps. Mrs. John R. Neeley, president of the auxiliary, unveiled the statue. Captain Rexroad, chaplain of the 161st infantry, delivered a brief eulogy of the flyer, while three national guard airplanes circled overhead, dropping flowers.

In a taped session at Bill Toth's "Old Timers" meeting in September 1978, Dwight Smith articulately told about some of his early experiences. He had learned to fly at Foster Russell Airport with instruction by Tom Symons. One of the other pilots there, Frank Campbell, had ground-looped his JN-4 (0x-5) and "washed out the bottom panels." Dwight bought the craft (cheap) and was able, with the help of friends, to find a spare set of "uppers" which they mated to the Jenny. This may sound routine but, when you remember the Jenny had a shorter lower wing span on the bottom set, you can see how the results were a little unique. Dwight's "new" JN-4 had both wings long with a good increase in lift area and a extra set of vertical struts on the outer ends between the wings. Although the plane had more lift, it also had more drag and could only make about 60 MPH max. He reports "it landed about 30 and was a fairly successful bird."

Dwight pointed out he was not one of the charter members of the 116th but he did join shortly afterwards. Since he had already piled up some time in his own ship, he had little trouble in passing the written exam and was commissioned a second lieutenant. He remembers well the 1925 air circus and crash and the very impressive and successful National Air Races and Air Derby that followed in 1927. Incidentally, when he joined the squadron in 1925 or 1926, "they had four Curtiss JN-6 (with 180 Hisso) and one DH-4" (with the Liberty). In 1926 interesting feats were being accomplished around the world by aircraft. Floyd Bennett flew Adm. Richard E. Byrd in a Fokker Tri-motor named *Josephine Ford* from Spitsbergen to the North Pole and returned. Several days later the dirigible *Norge*, with Roald Amundsen and Lincoln Ellsworth aboard, flew from the same spot over the pole and on to Alaska, thus satisfying those explorers who had failed in 1925.

Back at the Spokane Airport things were continuing to move forward. At this time the road that was the south boundary of the airport ran in an exact east-west line from Fancher Way (named later), where the National Guard hangars were, to the Waterworks Boulevard, rather than its later position paralleling the Spokane International tracks. This would place it in front (north) of what later became the Spokane Community College aero facility. Nick Mamer built his first inexpensive lean-to-type hangar on about the same spot and farther to the east one block, near the National Guard's old four-plane hangar, someone also built a similar hangar (which in 1928 belonged to Spokane Airways). Mamer's first and second hangars ran at right angles to the road. The other hangar was very close to and paralleling the railroad tracks. At this time all the hangars at the airport were painted a dark color except Mamer's second, which was white.

The most permanent construction during 1926 was the Guard's new operational headquarters. This fine brick structure was done in several parts, but the east wing, built during 1926, is the part that was later occupied by the FAA General Aviation office. Later, middle and west wings were added.

That "other" Owen, Bob that is, not Claude or Rus, made the headlines in the *Chronicle*:

OWEN PLANE HAS SECOND SMASH

National Guard Flyer Almost Wrecks Plane When Gas Gives Out. Pullman, Wash. April 6 Crashing the second time in 48 hours. Captain Robert Owen of the 116th national guard aerial squadron of Spokane, almost completely wrecked his guard airplane yesterday afternoon. Saturday Captain Owen went to Pullman on practice duty and while flying over the college grounds his gasoline supply ran out. He was forced to land in a plowed field. His ship nosed over and was damaged. Three mechanics from Spokane came here and repaired the machine yesterday and at 3 p.m. Captain Owen took to the air intending to go back to Spokane. Captain Owen had gained but a little altitude yesterday when his motor stopped and in making a landing he broke a wing of the plane, the propeller and other parts of the plane. Field repairs were impossible and the plane, in a truck, left here today for its base. Captain Owen and his passenger escaped both times without injury.

A 1926 publicity photo of a conference at Parkwater whereby officials appear to be making a deal with the fly-boys. The DH-4 may be the one used in the forest patrol work during the summer.

An account in the June 17th *Spokesman-Review* described typical activities of the 116th Squadron:

116TH AIR MEN OPEN THEIR CAMP – 85 Enlisted and 20 Officers Get Things in Shape at Parkwater – Their day starts at 5:30. Practice Squadron and Flying Formations and Technical Work -- Two Pass Exams

The establishment of mess systems, placing of parking signs, policing of areas, cleaning of arms and equipment and physical inspection occupied the time of most of the 85 enlisted men and 20 officers of the 116th observation squadron the first day of the second annual encampment at the Parkwater field yesterday. A few of the officers were up in planes learning flying formations, but most of the men were kept on the ground getting the camp ready for the remainder of the two weeks of active work. Buell Felts of Opportunity and William H. Williams, W. 2003 York, each received notification yesterday by telegram that they had passed their second lieutenant examinations.

Starting this morning, the men will be called at 5:30 each morning and will have half hour of calisthenics before breakfast. Inspections will start at 6:45 and special infantry drill will occupy the men till 9. The officers of the camp will practice squadron and flying formations each morning from 9 to 11:30 and the enlisted men will do technical work. During the afternoon the men will study theories of flight and have more technical work. An attempt will be made tomorrow by technical Sergeant Ed Craney to communicate with an airplane from the radio station at the field. Although this was attempted yesterday it was not entirely successful, and Sergeant Craney believes that Friday the test can be satisfactorily completed. Major D. C. Emmons of Crissey field, San Francisco: Major Bert Vanderwilt of Everett and Captain E. A. Easterbrook of Fort Wright held a conference with Major John Fancher, Commander of the encampment, yesterday morning.

On May 29, 1927, Lt. James Buell Felts was killed in an accident near the field. This was the second fatal crash at Parkwater and also involved a Jenny aircraft. As a result of this unfortunate happening, Major

Jack Fancher announced that the National Guard flying field at Parkwater would be named Felts Field, with official dedication to take place in September during the National Air Races, which Spokane had just been successful in landing. More on this later.

By the summer of 1927, the old Curtiss JN-6 training planes started to be replaced by the more modern consolidated PT-1 ships. The *Spokane Chronicle* on July 1st tells of the situation:

NEW TYPE PLANES FOR GUARD PILOTS – Two New Ships Assigned to Spokane Unit – Will be here For Air Races. Two new airplanes of the latest army training type known as the PT-1, and motored with a 180-horsepower Wright motor, will be delivered to the 41st division air service squadron at Felts Field, Parkwater, it was officially announced in a telegram received at the air port today from Colonel Syermyer, air service officer in command of national guard aviation affairs for the Ninth corps area with headquarters at San Francisco. Delivery of the planes, which are now ready for flight here from Rockwell Field, San Diego, will be made by Lieutenant C. V. Haynes, regular army instructor attached to the local squadron, who has been ordered to proceed by railroad to Rockwell field for the purpose of flying the ships to Parkwater. After delivering his first ship the lieutenant will return south for a second delivery. The same order states that we will not fly the "Jennie" planes after September 1," said Major Jack T. Fancher, commander of the 41st division air service. "The Jennies, which are the oldest type of army plane, will pass out of existence. The PT-1s are two-seaters, and are somewhat similar to the TW type of ship we now have here for a time. Our Jennies are to be replaced with the PT-1s and three observation planes of the Falcon type which have Liberty motors. The Falcons are also two-seaters. It is the hope of officers in the local flying unit that delivery will be possible of all five of the PT-1s and Falcons before the national air races here September 23 and 24 as there are several events in the national air races for national guard aviation ships only.

Nick Mamer (third from the right) and friends.

Lieutenant James Buell Felts, killed in a crash of a JN-6 at Parkwater in May 1927, was the squadron member for whom Felts Field was named.

Not all landings were smooth! Photos of a wreck by Lieutenant Felts, one mile south of the Parkwater airfield.

The Curtiss JN-6 (Hisso 180 HP) gave way to the Consolidated PT-1 (180 Hisso) for trainers.

The DH-4s were replaced by the more modern Douglas 02-H (with 450 HP Liberty engines). The first ones were painted blue with yellow wings, but later with olive drab fuselage.

The ships of the 116th Observation Squadron in February 1931. (From left) two Douglas 02-H (Liberty 400 HP), five Douglas 0-38 (Wright Cyclone 600 HP), two Consolidated PT-1 trainers (Wright Whirlwind 200 HP).

Squadron formation, 1932.
(Courtesy MAC L95-34.124, Washington Air National Guard, 116th Photo Section, Jack O'Brien Collection)

By 1931 the new Wright-powered Douglas 0-38 (foreground) were replacing the older Liberty powered 02-H aircraft (background).

A photo of the 116th with 12 (names only) of the 15 men identified: Captain Lawrence C. Sherman, Captain Ed Axberg, Captain Elmer E. Langley, Major Jack T. Fancher (front row center), Captain H. R. Neely, Captain Robert W. Owen, Lieutenant William H. Williams, Lieutenant Harold Peters, Lieutenant W. Wadsworth, Lieutenant Claude Owen, Lieutenant Hillford R. Wallace, Lieutenant Charles C. Holter.

Washington Governor Clarence Martin and some of the 116th officers in 1934.

The first Boeing B-17 visited the Felts Field headquarters of the Washington Air National Guard in 1941. (They also put it in the new hangar to see how it would fit.)

Lieutenant Harold Peters (left) and Sergeant Marcus Peters, both with the 116th Observation Squadron.

Major Hillford Wallace, second from right, and the brass, 1938.

"How am I going to explain this to the Old Man?"

The beloved Douglas 02-H with the 450 HP Liberty engine, 1931.

"I knew there was something fishy about that $2.00 air fare to Seattle!" Photo taken at Gray Field, Tacoma, Washington, circa 1939.

The National Air Derby and Air Races

Charles Lindbergh standing in front of his famous plane, the *Spirit of St. Louis.* **This photo was taken on May 31, 1927.** *(Photo courtesy Library of Congress)*

Nineteen twenty-seven was one of the most dynamic and epic-making years in aviation history. In May 1927, when Charles A. Lindbergh flew his *Spirit of St. Louis* across the Atlantic from New York to Paris, he started an avalanche of aeronautical progress that swept the world and eventually was to affect the lives of millions.

This quiet "American Boy" from Minnesota captured the hearts and imagination of all – young and old, male and female, rich and poor, aviation enthusiast and non-aviation enthusiast. After his famous 34-hour solo flight in a small single-engine monoplane, he was a world hero overnight. "Lucky Lindy" was on the lips of practically everyone, including the residents of Spokane.

He was exactly the right person at precisely the right time to open the eyes of the world to the tremendous potential of the airplane. He instilled a faith in its capability and its future that allowed the bungling young industry to grow and change the destiny of mankind.

I remember it well because I was 10 years old at the time and was in the fifth grade at the Hutton School in Spokane. For several years previously I had, like many other young boys (and some girls), been a student of aviation. I had followed the reports in the papers and magazines about the airmail pilots flying the mail, the giant dirigibles of the post World War I era, the thrilling accounts of the aviation pioneers as they progressed through those early years towards an uncertain future. I had already seen my first air show at the National Guard flying field at Parkwater and had on many Sunday mornings gone to the field to watch the activities of the 116th Observation Squadron. I liked what I saw. That was for me!

The fact the Lindbergh flight had enlightened the general public to the capability of the "modern" aircraft to span the oceans and, maybe the world, was a great help to Spokane when they tried to secure the National Air Races for 1927. This single event seemed to tip the young aviation industry off dead center and start it rolling to a then uncomprehendable future.

On Monday, September 12, 1927, Charles A. Lindbergh landed his *Spirit of St. Louis* in Spokane during his nationwide tour of 75 cities following his epic trans-Atlantic flight of May 21st. Dignitaries from the city, state and the military, as well as hundreds of ordinary admirers, greeted him at the airport. Only the grandstand at the fairgrounds were big enough to accommodate the larger crowds waiting to honor him and hear his speech. The day's festivities culminated in a banquet at the Davenport Hotel.

Charles Lindbergh giving a speech at the Spokane Fairgrounds on September 12, 1927. *(Courtesy MAC, Libby photo L87-1.34192.29)*

CHAPTER 5 – THE NATIONAL AIR DERBY AND AIR RACES

Before landing at Buell Felts Airfield (now known as Felts Field) at 2:04 that rainy afternoon, Lindbergh swooped "so low" over the old Interstate Fairgrounds (later Playfair Race Track) to greet the 20,000 awaiting his arrival that it was possible to read *Spirit of St. Louis* on its aluminum cowling. (The plane, built by the Ryan Aircraft Company of San Diego, was named in honor of St. Louis boosters who financed it.)

When the plane came into view, the welcoming committee at Felts Field had to clear the runway of the surging crowd so Lindbergh could land. The dignitaries on hand to greet him personally included Washington Air National Guard Commandant Major John T. "Jack" Fancher, Governor Roland H. Hartley, Mayor Charles A. Fleming, and Harlan I. Peyton, a Spokane investment tycoon who had been a flight instructor during World War I. The same men were busy promoting the National Air Races to be held in Spokane during the week of September 21st.

A limousine soon whisked Lindbergh to the fairgrounds, a few miles to the west, to the waiting throngs that included school children who had been dismissed for the day. Fortunately, the heavy rain and wind moderated to a drizzle in time for Lindbergh's speech, in which he asserted that aviation had come of age: "We have today advanced to a stage where the airplane is entirely practical. Commercial aviation compares in safety with all other forms of transportation." He emphasized that air mail, freight, and passenger service were now "proven uses for the airplane" and that commercial aviation, which was safe, should not be confused with stunt flying, experimental, and "pioneering aviation," as well as "distance flights," which were still inherently dangerous.

That evening, a banquet in the elegant Marie Antoinette Room of Spokane's Davenport Hotel was packed with 525 guests invited from the city and the Inland Northwest to honor Lindbergh. Harlan I. Peyton gave the welcome speech preceding Lindbergh's address. The celebrated aviator spent the night in the State Suite at the Davenport before resuming his national tour. Newspaper writer Ellsworth French recalled 25 years later that "Lindbergh did everything anyone asked him to do while here, including a low-level flight past St. Luke's Hospital so that crippled children in the Shrine Hospital could see the *Spirit of St. Louis*"

The Davenport menu and program in honor of Charles Lindbergh. *(Courtesy MAC)*

The enormous success of this event heightened excitement for the upcoming National Air Derby and Air Races scheduled for later the same month. Major Jack Fancher, chairman of the committee to organize and promote the event, had been in New York to greet Lindbergh upon his return from his trans-Atlantic flight in May. Of course he invited Lindbergh to be a guest at the Spokane's National Air Races scheduled to begin September 21st, but Lindbergh had to cancel. His September 12th appearance in Spokane more than made up for it.

Program

Toastmaster
Mr. John F. Davies

Invocation
Right Reverend Edward Makin Cross

Orchestral Selections
Miss Lillian Fredericks, *Conductor*

Mendelssohn Club
    (a) Rolling Down to Rio
    (b) The Bells of St. Mary

Address of Welcome to Colonel Lindbergh
Mr. Harlan I. Peyton

Address
Colonel Charles A. Lindbergh

Menu

Honey Dew and Cantaloupe Cocktail Supreme

Celery Hearts   Jumbo Olives   Salted Almonds

Clam Broth and Chicken Essence Bellevue
Paillettes au Parmesan

Roast Stuffed Imperial Squab on Raisin Toast
Le Bourget
Fresh Corn Pudding au Gratin
Sweet Potato Cakes Glace
Currant Jelly

Tomato, Asparagus Tips, Avocado, Diplomate

Coupe aux Marrons Lindbergh
Gateau Spirit of St. Louis

Demi-Tasse

CHAPTER 5 – THE NATIONAL AIR DERBY AND AIR RACES

Charles Lindbergh arrived in Spokane on September 12, 1927. Top: Major Jack Fancher, left, and Mayor Charles Fleming greet Lindbergh at Felts Field. Bottom: Dignitaries with Lindbergh.

NATIONAL AIR DERBY AND AIR RACES

Jack Fancher remembered that the 1925 Spokane Air Circus had been a big local success. However, in the two years previous to 1927, the cities of Los Angeles and Cleveland had rather dismal experiences trying to put on a national event. How then could a smaller community like Spokane expect to host one successfully? Well, Spokane had in that day a "live-wire" business community that was willing to put its money where its mouth was and an active Chamber of Commerce organization (not unlike the pre-Expo '74 era). In addition, the city had two outstanding aviation leaders in Jack Fancher and Nick Mamer. With the Lindbergh-precipitated worldwide aviation awakening, Spokane thought the project timely and looked forward to it with enthusiasm.

In July the committee sent Major Jack Fancher, managing director of the Air Derby Association of Spokane, to New York and back to make arrangements along the route and drum up enthusiasm. He was scheduled to leave on July 11th, but according the newspaper accounts, did not get underway until the morning of the 13th. The Libby Studio recorded in its ledger that they took several photographs at Felts Field on July 11th of Fancher's supposed send-off by dignitaries of the committee. Apparently, this photo opportunity was already scheduled and went ahead, showing Fancher entering another plane than the one he actually flew. According to newspaper accounts, he could not have made this trip in Nick Mamer's Swallow.

The Tuesday, July 12th *Spokane Press* stated:

> Another delay in the departure of Major John T. Fancher and Raymond A. Carroll on their cross-continent flight to New York in the interest of the National Air Derby race between New York and Spokane was made necessary today, when Lieutenant C. V. Haynes was forced down at Medford, Ore. with the PT-1 plane which Major Fancher will fly. . . .

Wednesday's *Spokesman-Review* reported: "Major John T. Fancher will take off for New York at 6:00 a.m. today in an army plane, he announced yesterday. He expected to leave Monday morning but was delayed by the non-arrival of the plane he wished to use . . . a PT-1 army plane . . . "

The *Spokesman-Review* for Thursday, July 14th, bore the headline "Fancher Flight East a Rapid One" and announced that the departure of Major Fancher and Sergeant Carroll took place at 7:10 the previous morning, but described the plane as a "Douglas plane with a new Liberty motor."

Nick Mamer had a sign painted on the side of one of his planes in order to publicize the National Air Derby and National Air Races wherever he flew. In the same cluster of photos the Libby Studio took on July 11th is one of Nick Mamer in a plane bearing such a sign in bold letters. This photo is sometimes identified as Mamer's famous Swallow. However, the *Spokesman-Review* of July 14th announced purchase the previous day of a "Whirlwind motored Swallow airplane to be flown as a Spokane entry in the National Air Derby race from . . . New York to Spokane by pilot N. B. Mamer. Mr. Mamer will accept delivery of the plane at the factory [in Wichita, Kansas] about September 1st." If this article is correct, a photo taken on July 11th could not have been the Swallow, nor could Fancher have used the Swallow for his cross-country flight beginning on July 13th. To further complicate matters, the paper states that the intention of the citizen-funded purchase of the Swallow, costing $10,000, was for Mamer to use in the race.

As it turned out, however, this plane was not flown by Nick Mamer and Bruce McDonald in the actual air races because it was underpowered and slow. Instead, the Buhl Aircraft Company, with some money from the local committee, furnished a more powerful and capable Wright J-5 powered open-cockpit biplane for the Spokane entry. Nick and Bruce finished third in the Class A event from New York City.

CHAPTER 5 – THE NATIONAL AIR DERBY AND AIR RACES

The *Spokesman-Review*, Sunday, September 18, 1927, disclosed detailed plans for the upcoming event:

WORLD'S PREMIER AIR EVENTS WILL BE HELD IN SPOKANE THIS WEEK – Spokane men landed meet. General Committee Representative of City's interests. The Spokane General Committee which engineered the Air Derby and Races consisted of Walter Evans, Victor Dessert, Charles Hebberd, Major John T. Fancher, W. H. Cowles, Harlan 1. Peyton, John W. Graham, Frank R. Culbertson, Milton McGoldrick, Col. Thomas G. Aston, Glen Pattee, L. M. Davenport, Clyde Johnson, E. E. Flood, S. A. Mitchell, H. W. Pierong, Frank Davies, Ray Grombacker, Guy Toombes, Leon J. Boyle, Ellsworth French, Don Babcock, P. J. Garnett, E. S. McPherson, Ray Dahl, Leo Brooks, Harold Neely, Lloyd Hill, William Burrow. (They are the chief underwriters of the big air meet this week.)

Details were handled by the Executive Committee of the National Air Derby Association. These include: Walter Evans-President; Victor Dessert and Harlan Peyton-Vice President; Charles Hebberd Treasurer; Col. T. G. Aston; Leon J. Boyle; W. H. Cowles; H. W. Pierong and W. H. Ude. James Ford is acting as executive secretary and Ellsworth C. French publicity director. Major John T. Fancher, commanding officer of the 41st Division, Air Service, has been managing director. Other details were handled by a number of active sub-committees.

RAISE MORE THAN $60,000 – Spokane backers of Air Meet gave time and many hours of work in committee, morning, afternoon and evenings, holidays and Sundays included, with breakfast, luncheons, dinners and banquets being given by a comparatively small group of Spokane businessmen to assure the success of the National Air Derbies and National Air Races. They had been quietly at work for weeks before the announcement was made last May that the National Aeronautics Association had awarded the races to Spokane and had sanctioned the proposed air derbies. Since June 1, this group, in part or in whole, has hardly missed a day without a conference of some nature. Often the sessions

Nick Mamer planes and his ad promotion, 1927.

ran two or three hours long and entailed much work that had to be done in addition to the time given to the conference. They raised more than $60,000 in record time.

NATIONAL AIR DERBIES ARE TO BRING 70 FAST RACING PLANES Sometime Wednesday afternoon September 21, the planes in the two national air derbies from New York to Spokane should drop in at the Spokane Airport. The spectacle is full of dramatic possibilities. At least 70 planes are expected to compete in the various derbies. The San Francisco planes will start that morning and with a brief stop at Swan Island Airport, Portland, should easily reach Spokane at mid-afternoon. Six planes are officially entered.

The Class B, or slower planes, from New York will be started off from Roosevelt Field, New York, Monday morning and the stops, both short and overnight, are so timed as to bring them into Spokane Wednesday afternoon. There are 32 of them.

While the Class A, or faster planes, leave New York a day later, they should almost catch up to the slower planes because they make fewer stops and fly much faster. Their schedule should bring them in during the afternoon. There are 18 planes in this event. The nonstop planes from New York will not leave New York until Wednesday afternoon between 2 and 4 o'clock, eastern time, or 10 and 12 o'clock Spokane time. There will be at least 6 starting. Lindbergh thinks some of them will make the 2400 miles in 24 hours, but Thursday afternoon should see most of them in Spokane, if the weather permits them to start on scheduled time. Their progress will be heralded by radio and telegraph.

OFFER $63,250 TO WINNERS OF EVENTS – Cash prizes, aggregating $63,250 together with trophies valued at $10,000, will be competed for in the National Air Derbies and the National Air Races at the Spokane Airport this week. The National Air Derbies will take $48,250 of the cash and the Air Races $15,000 in addition to $10,000 in trophies. MILITARY FLYERS IN FORCE =Army, Navy, Marine Corps, National Guard and Reserve Corps flyers will be on hand in force. Pilots in the service are not permitted to compete for cash prizes, but they will be out in strength for the events where trophies are offered and for others for which they can qualify. San Diego, Crissy Field, Quantico, Pearson Field and Selfridge Field will be represented.

And so went the advance publicity for the Air Derby. The way I remember it as an interested, and indirectly involved ten-year-old, is still indelible in my mind. Our company, McGoldrick Lumber, had a "box" in the front row of the temporary grandstand erected on a diagonal line starting just east of the Guard hangars. Each box had about eight or ten chairs and the structure extended several hundred feet along the south edge of the flying field activity center. My father and other company officials invited some of their customers and friends to join them for the activities. Things were happening much of the time during the week that preceded the official program. For example, Lt. Jimmy Doolittle of the U.S. Army Air Corps was a tremendous favorite with the Spokane people. He was flying the latest Curtiss Hawk (P-1) modified for inverted flight and racing and during the week he was preparing his ship and routine for the performance. The Hawk was really "boisterous!" It had a 600-HP Curtiss V-12 engine (Curtiss Conqueror) which had four valves per cylinder, overhead cams, and with 12 short exhaust stacks out each side. Twenty-four of them naked, so-to-speak, and coming out of 1,500 plus cubic inches usually with the throttle against the firewall. All this power (and noise) was hitched to a fixed pitch metal propeller whose tips were traveling at a tip speed just under the speed of sound in order to maintain propeller efficiency, but at a velocity that really churned up the sound waves! When a P-1 flew by the grandstand in a maximum performance low pass, it really attracted attention! A virtual audio earthquake happened as the plane approached the observer, with a rapidly increasing whine that crescendoed into a deafening complex wave-shape sound that would make the present-day teenager's automotive stereo seem like a falling goose feather. The climactic acoustical experience was when the plane passed directly in front of you and the full effect of the prop noise and the exhaust sound combined together for an instant and then faded rapidly into the past, leaving some younger red-blooded observers contemplating a trip to the Air Corps recruiting office.

Now if you take this kind of sound and mix it with the most beautiful aircraft and the most daring acrobatic flying you have a combination sure to bring people to the 1927 Air Show. Part of the build-up for the big three days of races, stunts and performances happened in just this manner. Lt. Jimmy Doolittle of the U.S.

Pre-race publicity for the National Air Races and National Air Derby.

Army Air Corps, Lt. Al Williams of the U.S. Navy, and Lt. Yolemans for the Marine Corps – all had Curtiss Hawks and were to compete on Saturday. During the preliminary days they would take their planes out for a spin and practice up on whatever acrobatic pilots practice up on. Doolittle had only recently invented the outside loop (where the head is on the outside) and was later to set the world's record for continuous outside loops, which, as I recall, was about eight or nine. Several years later, Tex Rankin in a Great Lakes Trainer set the record with 39 consecutive outside loops before his eyeballs or something else gave out. Needless to say, boys will be boys, and much of the preparation was done over downtown Spokane with disrupting results. After Jimmy flew inverted down Riverside (probably several hundred feet above the Old National Bank Building), people ran out into the street with their eyes and mouths open, whereby the young ace proceeded to give them a little taste of what was going to happen at Felts on the morrow. The icing on the promotional cake was when the commanding officer was rumored to have "grounded the young daredevil" and prevented him from flying again until the next day when the official program was to begin. With all this excitement in September of 1927, almost all of Spokane went to the airport whenever they could. Because school had started, we school kids could not wait to get out there on Saturday and see firsthand what the grown-ups were talking and laughing about at the dinner table.

One sidelight was how the members of the committee and the Chamber of Commerce acted as hosts to the

Women mailing posters for the National Air Races to be held in Spokane, September 21-25, 1927. (*Courtesy MAC, Libby detail of Libby photo L87-1.34067-27*)

CHAPTER 5 – THE NATIONAL AIR DERBY AND AIR RACES

This Fireside Edition of the September 21, 1927, front page article in the *Spokane Daily Chronicle* emphasizes the significance of the National Air Derby to Spokane's history. At the time of this article, the size of this newspaper was 18 x 22 inches. With the exception of 12 column inches, the entire front page was devoted to aviation. The immediate caption under the drawing states: "Speeding westward to Spokane from New York are the entrants in the Class 'A' and Class 'B' National Air Derby races. The *Chronicle* has prepared this map that every one may visualize the race. Each little plane is numbered and, by referring to the list of entrants below, the reader can keep an accurate check of the progress of the races. Planes forced down are turned nose downward."

The majority of this 20-page newspaper was also devoted to aviation and this event. Page ten contained an article that described the state of public excitement in Spokane: "Spokane followed Colonel Lindbergh's advice today and became "air minded" in every sense of the word. As the cross-continent racers from New York neared the Spokane airport, stock brokers abandoned their tickers, businessmen their desks, clerks their counters, housewives their kitchens and washerwomen their tubs to get the latest news of the progress of the flight. . . . A majority of downtown stores closed after 1 p.m., giving employers and employees alike an opportunity to witness the finish of the derbies and the thrilling program of the aeronautic events at the field during the afternoon." . . . "The police were taxed to the limit handling traffic on the downtown streets. Hundreds of cars from Inland Empire points, as well as from cities in distant states, are here for the air events."

visitors each evening during the week. The three services of the military had tents set up at Felts Field and some of the enlisted specialists stayed there with the equipment. The military pilots stayed at the local hotels and homes, as did the commercial and sport participants. One night at our home, on 26th and Rhyolite Road, there were a number of guests, including a Lt. Irvin Woodring, U.S. Army Air Corps, whose calling card I kept for years, hoping all the time that someday I would also go to Kelly Field and become a pilot.

The air races consisted of several races beginning in New York and San Francisco and ending in Spokane. Various classes of aircraft, some fast, some slower, competed for cash prizes and trophies. Many cities and companies throughout the nation sponsored planes and pilots. Military planes also participated, but were not eligible for cash prizes. Charles W. "Speed" Holman of Minneapolis won the $10,000 purse Class A race from New York in which Nick Mamer, with Bruce McDonald as observer, flew a Wright J5-powered open-cockpit Buhl biplane for the Spokane entry to come in third. Washington Air National Guardsmen Tom Symons and Alphonse Coppula won the race for National Guard pilots and planes. Winners received their trophies from queen for the event, Vera McDonald Cunningham.

The most visible parts of the program were the events at Felts Field. There was competition of all types between the various military teams, a close formation, precision acrobatic performance by the three inter-service aces mentioned above, as well as individual performances of all the "greats" of U.S. aviation. I saw my first little Buhl "Bullpup," a novel single-seater monoplane with a three cylinder, air-cooled engine and aluminum fuselage. Also, Edward Bavard Heath in his tiny Heath Parasol, a very light monoplane made from a kit, gave an interesting demonstration and, at the end, picked up the tail skid and pulled the plane off the field. One guy doing a loop came out a little late and hit the ground hard enough to lose a wheel that bounced over into the crowd, fortunately without injuring anyone seriously. Right now I can close my eyes and look down the line of planes and remember several at the east end. There was a Hamilton metal monoplane with a single engine and corrugated metal skin like the Ford Tri-motor, and a Ryan B-I Brougham similar to Lindbergh's *Spirit of St. Louis* but the regular model with J-5 and 5 place. It apparently belonged to the Maxwell House Coffee Company and was perpetuated in my mind because it had a picture of a large coffee cup held up as if to drain, and the words "Good to the Last Drop" were painted on each side of the fuselage. One of the memorable performances was the looping of a tri-motored Ford transport plane by one of the nationally famous visiting pilots. All the then currently known aeronautical skills and equipment were demonstrated.

Looking back on it, the whole event was a great success: Everybody was a winner in one way or another, and Spokane became known as a leader in our nation for aviation activity for the first time. The National Air Races in the years that followed were then successfully held in Cleveland and Los Angeles, and the country went forward into the air age. Spokane had a part of it!

A brief summary of statistics illustrates Spokane's successful event:

    Number of paid admissions............................ 99,199
    Attendance at one time..................................... 20,000
    Funds raised by private subscription $76,625
    Prize money offered ....more than $60,000
    Scheduled cross-country races from
        New York City.............................. 2275 miles
      Non-stop (non-military)
      Class A (two-place stock)

Class B (smaller, low-powered)
from San Francisco..................... 925 miles
Scheduled closed-course speed dashes for military
(interservice) 10-mile triangular course, 6 and 12 laps.
Committee's expenses over income................... none

An additional sidelight, as I glance down the list of the members of the Committee for the Air Derby, many were well known to me at the time. Vic Dessert of the Dessert Hotel and his wife Georges (Wilson) and daughters Mary Louise "Marilu" and Joan were our family's closest friends. We all grew up together during the years, much like brother and sisters. Charlie Hebberd was the secretary/ treasurer of the Tull and Gibbs Home Furnishings store located in the same block as the Dessert Hotel on First Avenue and Wall Street. (The Jones and Dillingham Paint Store was in between.) Major Jack Fancher, capable commanding officer of the 116th Observation Squadron of the Washington Air National Guard, is well-documented elsewhere in this text.

William H. Cowles Sr. was the publisher of the *Spokesman-Review* and the *Spokane Daily Chronicle* and had numerous other interests. He and R. L. Rutter of the Spokane and Eastern Bank and certain other business leaders could always be depended upon to do their part financially to promote aviation in Spokane.

Harland Peyton was the son of "Colonel" Peyton, early Spokane pioneer and associated with the Peyton Building on Post between and Sprague and Riverside.

Some of the members of the Executive Committee of the Air Derby Association met with Major Fancher, third from left, at Parkwater in preparation for the big airshow, 1927. *(Courtesy MAC, Libby Photo L87-1.33747-27)*

John W. Graham was the founder of the company of the same name, which was for some time Spokane's leading stationery house. Their slogan was "If It's Made of Paper, We Have It."

Frank Culbertson had a fine department store across the street from the present Parkade in the Welch Building, part of which is now Macy's (formerly the Bon Marche).

Milton McGoldrick, my father, was then the secretary/treasurer of the McGoldrick Lumber Company, President of McGoldrick-Sanderson Company (Firestone tire distributors) and involved in several other smaller concerns.

Louis Davenport, of the Davenport Hotel, was on the Old National Bank board of directors with my grandfather, J. P. McGoldrick, and later on the same board with my father. (Our company, the McGoldrick Lumber Company, was the last major stockholder of the Davenport Hotel to sell its interest in the hotel back to Mr. Davenport so that he became sole owner in the 1920s.)

Ed Flood was president of the Exchange National Bank at Howard and Riverside, across the street from the Spokane and Eastern. He lived on Rockwood Boulevard and Upper Terrace and his kids went to the Hutton School with us.

Harry W. "Nick" Pierong was manager of the Pantages Theater on Howard Street between Riverside and Main. Nick and his wife, Maime, were good friends of Mom and Dad. The Pantages was a beautiful theater and specialized in vaudeville acts that moved throughout the national chain of theaters of the same name. The Pierongs did not have any children of their own, therefore the Dessert kids and my sister and I called them Uncle Nick and Aunt Maime.

Ray Grombacher owned the Liberty Theater on Riverside just west of the former Crescent Store. The Liberty Theater I remember well because it was the place I saw the first partial sound movie. At this time Warner Brothers' "Vitaphone" sound was based on a silent film with a separate large round record which was supposed to be more or less in sync with the picture. The first movie with this new system was *Tenderloin* starring Conrad Nagle. It made an impression on me because my mother, during her younger days, occasionally played the piano for silent films in a small movie theater. The bigger theaters had pipe organs. Shortly after the introduction of Vitaphone, a better process known as Movietone started appearing in the Fox Movietone News films. This process had a sound track on the film and was the beginning of the sound movies we have had ever since.

Guy Toombes was the manager of the Davenport Hotel for a number of years and later became manager of the Utah Hotel in Salt Lake City. Leon Boyle was a well-liked and active person and was the owner of the Boyle Fuel Company.

Ellsworth French wrote for the newspaper and was information officer for the 116th Squadron at Felts Field.

P. J. "Phillie" Garnett was a very colorful and often profane owner of the Universal Auto Company, which sold Ford and Lincoln autos. He also was somewhat involved with the sale of Ford Tri-motor airplanes to Sam Wilson of Spokane Airways and Cip Paulsen (Nick Mamer). Phillie was short with curved back and thick glasses, a big voice and a pretty blond wife named Madge. I could tell many humorous stories about him and his good friend Ray Ruhle at Liberty Lake.

Nick Pierong, manager of the Pantages Theater, holds a sterling silver service set to be won by some lucky military pilot.

E. S. "Eddie" McPherson was the dapper president of the Spokane International Railroad, built by D. C. Corbin to connect the Canadian Pacific with the Spokane transcontinental lines (it was later taken over by Fred Rummel).

The queen of the Air Derby was Vera McDonald Cunningham, who was married to Joe Cunningham. She was selected to be the official hostess and present the trophies because of her charm and ability to sell many advance tickets.

More than anyone else, Major Jack Fancher, Spokane's most beloved aviator, deserves credit for the success of the Spokane Air Races. Less than a year later, on April 28, 1928, Fancher was killed in a freak bomb blast. Major Fancher had taken his 41st Division, Air Service Unit to the Apple Blossom Festival in Wenatchee to participate in the activities there and spread the good word about flying and the National Guard. The accident occurred on the air field after he had completed a night flight during which he had dropped several bombs. He made a soft landing, went to his tent and changed into his uniform, then returned to his plane and took from the cockpit three bombs that were left over.

According to eyewitnesses, he remarked, "What's the matter with these things? Some of those I dropped failed to go off." With that, he took a scratcher in his left hand and tested two of the bombs, tossing them across the field. One exploded and the other failed to explode. The third bomb was discharged the instant he scratched it. There was a blinding flash and Major Fancher was seen to be reeling in a cloud of smoke. "My God, boys! What's happened?" He demanded, and fell in a heap. His right eye had been gouged out, his right hand blown off at the wrist, his body stripped bare above the waist. His torso was scorched and burned, and a metal button had been driven into the body cavity, injuring his liver.

He was driven to the hospital in a car by Lt. Jack Allenberg and several others and was fully conscious at all times. It is reported that he remarked, "Well, boys, I've made my last flight, and I am glad it was a night flight, but I'll still be able to handle a team on the farm, I guess." He raised his right arm to wipe away the sweat on his forehead and noticed that his hand was gone.

The news article further reported that "not a groan or word of his pain escaped the brave man during the trip to the hospital." He told the attending physician the details of the accident. He was given an anesthetic and the injured arm and eye were treated. Later in the night Jack lapsed into unconsciousness and died before dawn.

The untimely accident had a deep emotional effect on his officers and men in the squadron, on his many pilot buddies and on the people of Spokane and the state who had learned to respect and admire his genuine leadership.

Jack Fancher was born on the 1,400-acre wheat farm at Espanola near Medical Lake that he was operating at the time of his death. He would have been 37 years old on May 13th. He attended the old South Central High School in Spokane and graduated in June 1912. He was reported to be "one of the best athletes turned out there." He was end on the football team, "a mountain of strength" on the track team, but basketball was his particular forte.

Fancher later attended the University of Washington where he was a member of SAE fraternity and became one of the best basketball players in the conference and was captain of the university team.

When the United States entered World War I, he immediately joined the Aviation Corps, took his ground school at Berkeley and his flying at North Island, San Diego. He was sent overseas as a captain early in 1918 and was in command of a flying field at Chatillon Sur Seine until the Armistice.

As managing director of the National Air Derby the previous summer, he had flown across the United States over the route of the Derby to promote and give publicity to the event. He was warmly received by President Coolidge at the summer White House in Rapid City, South Dakota, during his journey.

He was survived by his wife, his father, two brothers and four sisters. In November 1928, a new airways beacon called Fancher Memorial Beacon was placed in service on top of "Fancher Hill" just north of Felts Field. The main road leading from the field to East Sprague was renamed from Hardesty Road to Fancher Way and a drinking fountain was dedicated in his honor. Over 1,000 cars were at the field during the ceremonies, and Ed Robertson, who was the father of Mrs. Tom (Ellen) Porter, an eloquent local lawyer spoke in high praise of the departed first commander of the Guard unit. Lt. C. V. Haynes, the Regular Army instructor of the Forty-first Division Air Unit (116 Observation Squadron of the Washington National Guard, was promoted to major and became the new commanding officer.

By the mid-thirties, the Department of Commerce had completed the installation of a series of rotating beacon lights along the national airways. This, combined with the four-course A-N radio range equipment and two-way radio, made night flying in good weather relatively safe and practical. In Spokane we had several beacon installations to guide the pilots to our fair city long before the national airways were completely lit. The most powerful of these was placed on the roof of the Old National Bank Building, which is 15 stories high. I forget how many hundred thousand candle-power it was claimed to be, but I do remember being able to see from the ground the effects of its very strong beam of light flash against the clouds, as far out as Coeur d'Alene under certain conditions. Pilots in the air observed its strong flash for more than 100 miles, except when the weather was bad.

A photo of Jack Fancher while serving in France during World War I, 1918. He was in command of a flying field at Chatillon Sur Seine.

This latter problem gave rise to a very unique beacon in Spokane. In the mid-twenties neon signs were just beginning to appear on storefronts and theaters downtown. At first they were only red, later blue and then green. They were somewhat of a novelty and our family would periodically take a drive after dinner to see the colorful new signs. Apparently some pilot coming in mentioned how he had seen a bright neon light one night when the weather was marginal and an ambitious salesman sold the Davenport Hotel on the idea of installing a red neon light on top of the west KHQ radio tower, which was then on the hotel roof. The design had a series of vertical red neon tubes about five feet tall and a circular layout. It was supposed to "cut through the fog," which of course it did not do. The strange thing about the whole story is that it remained for a number of years on top of the hotel weakly flashing away, completely forgotten by the numerous owners of the hotel who also probably did not know how to turn the power off! It is no longer in place atop the restored Davenport.

Our third and most practical beacon was the "Fancher Beacon" located on "Fancher Hill" just north of the Felts Field Airport, which is on Fancher Way and Rutter Avenue. This memorial to Jack Fancher was dedicated and turned on November 12, 1928, in an impressive ceremony attended by several thousand friends and dignitaries. Its location was more suitable for a rotating beacon than the Old National Bank. The beacon there was discontinued, while the Fancher light remained to perform its service to pilots for years and, to those who knew him, remind them of a great guy who lived too short a life. Now, too, the Fancher light is gone but not the memory of Jack Fancher.

The military escort at Major Fancher's funeral, May 1928. *(Photo courtesy General Wallace)*

During the 1929 outboard racing season, I received a letter from my favorite next-door neighbor, George Pedicord, who was ten years older than I and who was doing what I hoped to do when I grew up: taking flight training at March Field. George and my cousin Lucille were just about the best young swimmers (and "free board" riders) at Liberty Lake.

His older brother, Joe, was the speedboat king at Liberty Lake after my Uncle Ed retired from racing. In his letter George tells how it was at flight school:

> Yes, I heard about Joe winning at Sandpoint. Wish I could be there to ride a bit, but I am satisfied here with this. More fun, bigger and better thrills every day! If I can only stay to go to Kelly Field, I will be very lucky. We leave for Kelly the first of November. I mean those that are left. Now we have 64 out of 144 that started five months ago. They work them out pretty fast and send them home.
>
> When you asked me to write and tell you all about it here, it would mean a month's job! However, I'll try and give you an idea, if you can read my handwriting. The first four months were spent in learning to fly the primary ships "Consolidated PT-3's". It was great sport, especially acrobatics. Learned loops, spins, stalls, rolls, half rolls, etc., which was a job. Then we started on De Havillands. Oh yes, the PT's were powered with Wright Whirlwinds and very safe and over-powered. The DH-'s have Liberties and when you open it up it nearly deafens you.
>
> Last Monday I was among the lucky 10 and started on Douglas O-2K's. Soloed one yesterday and they are certainly a wonderful ship! Flying is just among the things we do. The ground school is the bunk. Flunk one subject and they send you home. Engineering subjects (and they keep me humping), then inspections and drills, etc. No time to relax at all! A very good description of the "Life of a Flying Cadet" can be found in the July issue of *Aero Digest*. It surely fits the subject. Well, Jim, one can never tell when he will be sent home so I may see you soon.
>
> Your old pal, G. W. Pedicord

CHAPTER 5 – THE NATIONAL AIR DERBY AND AIR RACES

A couple of months later, I was shocked to read in the paper the following dispatch:

SPOKANE AVIATOR KILLED IN CRASH
George Pedicord, 23, dies at March Field was in practice formation.

Practically on the eve of his graduation from the Regular Army Flying School at March Field, Riverside, Cal., Cadet George W. Pedicord, son of Minnie M. Pedicord and brother of Joe Pedicord, manager of the Pedicord Hotel, was killed in an airplane crash while flying formation today. His mother is in Riverside, having gone there for his graduation, which would have made him a lieutenant in the Air Corps, October 11.

Cadet Pedicord's ship locked wings in mid-air with a plane flown by Cadet P. B. Balfour, who joined the Caterpillar Club by leaping safely in his parachute. For some unknown reason, Pedicord did not resort to the chute, but went down with the wreckage.

The ships were biplanes, and it is believed the crash resulted from a malfunction of distance in making a steep bank. Pedicord, formerly was a private in the 41st Division Air Service Unit, Washington National Guard, having enlisted October 12, 1928. He was discharged February 19 for the purpose of enlisting in the Regular Army, thereby gaining admission to the flying school. Young Pedicord attended Lewis and Clark High School, and was an outstanding athlete in swimming and boxing. At the military camp, he recently won high honors in both events.

Early this afternoon, Joe Pedicord could not be located for notification of his brother's death.

Military officers from the 41st Division Air Services at Felt's Field, circa 1927. The biplane in the background was similar to the one involved in Pedicord's death. *(Bamonte collection)*

A typical Flying-V formation, dangerously close, but common during that time period. *(Bamonte collection)*

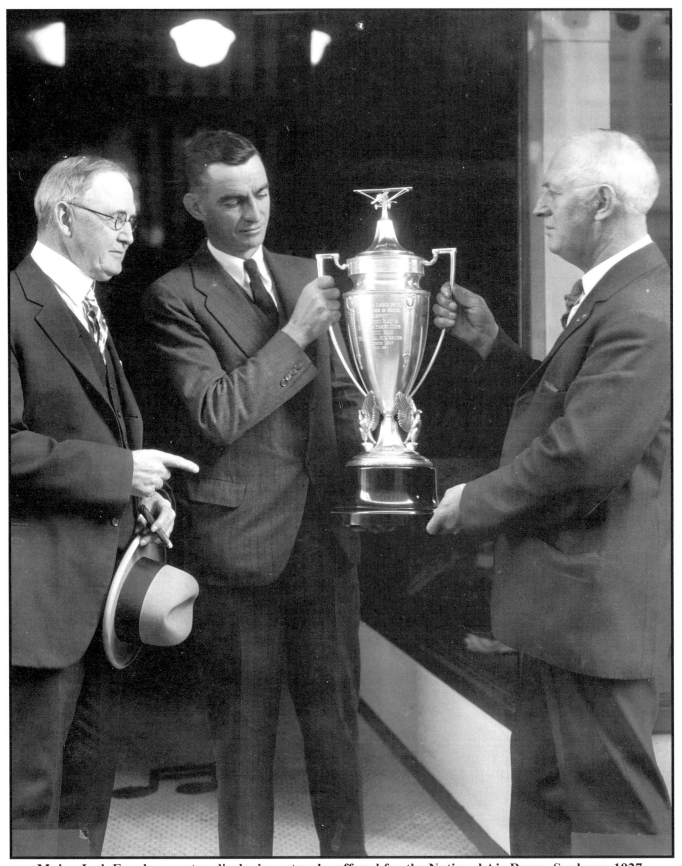
Major Jack Fancher, center, displaying a trophy offered for the National Air Races, Spokane, 1927.

The *Seattle Times* trophy for the winner of the Military Pursuit race at the National Air Races, Spokane, 1927.

Trophy offered by *Aero Digest* magazine for the National Guard pilots and planes race, National Air races. This trophy was won by Lt. Tom Symons and Al Coppula of the 116th Observation Squadron, Washington Air National Guard.

Michelangelo would have had a hard time outdoing the unique *Detroit News* Air Transport perpetual trophy won in 1927 by the Hamilton all-metal, aluminum monoplane.

Getting ready for the big show!

All the benches they could borrow from the local park department – and more – were placed behind the box seats.

Looking west from the judges' stand at some of the aircraft in the military area during the week before the races.

Some of the crowd before the program. The park benches formed the grandstand behind the reserved "boxes."

CHAPTER 5 – THE NATIONAL AIR DERBY AND AIR RACES

Part of the area behind the grandstand at Felts Field during the 1927 Air Derby.

Derby Queen Vera (McDonald) Cunningham presenting the winners with a special bouquet of roses shaped like an airplane. *(Courtesy MAC, Libby photo L87-1.34371)*

Handsome winner of $10,000 first place in Class A from New York, Charles W. "Speed" Holman. The aircraft he flew was a Laird with Wright Whirlman.

Mr. L. J. Shields, President of National Lead Battery Company, stands beside his Laird two-passenger biplane *National Eagle.* **It was powered by a Wright J-4 220 HP engine and flown by "Speed" Holman (with Sgt. Tom Lane) to win first prize in Class A in the New York to Spokane Air Derby in September 1927.**

An aerial view looking north. The small white objects along the river were "dummy" buildings which were bombed by the military in a spectacular demonstration.

Looking east with military tents along the flight line at the west end.

A specially prepared Curtiss XP-6A flown by Lt. Eugene Batten was the fastest plane timed around the pylons at 201.239 MPH, winning first place. Note the low drag appearance due to the flush radiators built into the upper wing rather than the regular P-1 tunnel design. (Engine was a souped up to 700 HP Curtiss "Conqueror" V-12.) Note the thin, straight wings.

Another aerial view of Air Derby activities at Felts Field.

A similar treatment for different Curtiss XP-6 type ship. Note sweep back of upper wing. It finished second in the speed contests.

The Marines brought this air-cooled radial-powered experimental plane, which was patterned after the Curtiss V-12 water-cooled "Hawk."

Top photos: competition for the Curtiss Hawk was the Boeing Pursuit plane. Bottom photo: a Marine Curtiss P-1. Note radiator under the engine and tapered wings.

Lt. Irvin Woodring, in the parachute, visited our home during the Air Derby and left his card, much to the pride of one 10-year-old boy.

A Curtiss P-1 Hawk.

The Navy and Marine pursuit planes in Spokane for the inter-service competition and demonstrations. Navy Lt. Al Williams was here and later became famous in the American Snyder Cup racing seaplane challenger. (His Packard X-24 powered racer failed to leave the water at 200-plus.)

"The cream of the crop." The nationally famous Jimmy Doolittle is on the far left.

Winners of the six-lap, 60-mile race around a triangular closed course for National Guard planes. Lt. Tom Symons and Al Coppula of the 116th Observation Squadron, Washington Air National Guard.

Walter Evans (left) welcomes Charlie Meyers to Spokane. Meyers flew this Class B racer an OX-5 WACO belonging to Tom Colby.

Eddie Ballough's Laird aircraft placed second in Class A from New York. Prize – $3,000 cash. The passenger with him was C. Dickinson.

"Tex" Rankin was here also in a WACO OX-5 ship. He saw Lt. Jimmy Doolittle perform the outside loop in the Curtiss Hawk and on November 19, 1934, broke the world record for continuous outside loops in his Great Lakes trainer.

Nick Mamer stands alongside his Buhl biplane that he and passenger Bruce McDonald flew for a third place finish in the Class A from New York. Prize – $2000.

Conference with Curtiss Army Team Specialist regarding XP-6 closed course racer.

The little Heath Parasol monoplane sits in front of the mighty Curtiss "Hawk" P-1.

The Class A winner from New York, Speed Holman, arrived at Felts Field with a blown left tire. Sgt. Tom Lane was his passenger.

A Curtiss P-1 Hawk.

Among the visitors were: McDaneld's Packard Special (top), Art Borne's Braun Special (second from bottom), and Lamb's Oriole (bottom).

Also in attendance were, second from bottom, Norman Goddard's *Gypsy*.

Parachute jumpers had their part in the show.

This was a very complex instrument panel in the RYAN M-1, *Pacific Air Transport* (P.A.T.).

The press photographers and newsreel cameramen were also in attendance.

National Air Races, 1927, Ellsworth French, publicity director. *(Courtesy MAC, Libby photo L94-24.121)*

Eddie Stinson and his famous Stinson monoplane *Miss Veedol*, which failed to reach Spokane nonstop from New York and had to land in Montana due to head winds that caused fuel exhaustion. (This plane was well known in 1927 when it was being prepared for the trans-ocean hop.)

Pilot "Duke" Schiller and his big Stinson monoplane *Royal Windsor* also ran out of fuel over Montana in the nonstop race from New York! This ship was prominent in early trans-Atlantic race activities. (Windsor is across the river from Detroit.)

John Miller, pilot, atop the early model Hamilton "Metal plane," which won the impressive *Detroit News* Air Transport trophy for highest efficiency. The man in the foreground is Tom Hamilton.

Vance Breese in a 1926 Stinson "Detroiter" biplane with a J-5 engine. (Stinson's first attempt at inside-pilot design.)

From the McGoldrick Company box at the front of the grandstand looking toward the flying field.

Felts Field, National Air Races, September 21-25, 1927. *(Courtesy MAC, David C. Guilbert photo L94-24.119)*

The Maxwell House Coffee Ryan B-1 at Felts Field during the National Air Races, September, 1927.

A few airplanes did get "bruised" during the show, but fortunately there were no serious injuries.

CHAPTER 5 – THE NATIONAL AIR DERBY AND AIR RACES

Look! I told you to watch out for that cow.

Charles Libby Jr. (with a press badge) arrived in a late model "Hisso" Standard and a suit that shows the rigors of extended open cockpit cross-country air travel. (He also forgot to take his goggles off.)

Chapter VI

The Tin Goose Era

Mamer Air Transport's *West Wind II* westbound over Spokane in 1930. East of the Division Street Bridge, the Spokane River meanders upriver toward Felts Field. The white smoke and steam rising from McGoldrick Lumber Co. sawmill is in the center foreground, with Gonzaga University just behind.

One of the most interesting and admired aircraft in Spokane commercial aviation circles during the late twenties and early thirties was the famous Ford Tri-motor. It was affectionately (and appropriately) called the "Tin Goose," because it was one of the new breed of all metal-construction planes becoming popular on the American scene, and because it was noisy inside.

The Ford 4-AT was a good airplane and considered big in its day, with 74 feet of span, 50 feet of length, a wheel tread of almost 17 feet, three Wright Whirlwind J-6 300-HP engines and an impressive five tons plus loaded! It could carry 11 passengers plus crew in comfortable wicker chairs at 110 MPH for more than 500 miles in a cabin 16 feet long with stand-up head room and a "washroom" of 68 cubic feet. More than 250 gallons of fuel and 30 gallons of oil were carried. Starters were the then common Bendix inertia hand-crank type.

It is interesting to trace just how this "Pride of the Skies" came to be, how it got the Ford name on the side, and why it looks so much like the Fokker. Back in 1923, a young inventor named William B. Stout induced a group of eastern businessmen to back him in a venture to build a "modern" transport plane. Heading the list of backers (that read like the *Who's Who in America*) were the names of Henry and Edsel Ford. The Stout Metal Airplane Co. was formed and its first experimental aircraft was a four-place turkey with a Curtiss 90-HP OX-5 engine and was called the "Air Sedan." After the first test (in the presence of the board of directors), the disappointed William Stout, never at a loss for words, told Mr. Ford that what he needed was "more money to buy more horsepower." Henry Ford looked at the plane and said, "You don't need more money, son, you need more airplane!"

A financial arrangement was made with the Fords supplying the money and Bill Stout designing and building a pretty good all-metal high-wing airplane with a single Liberty 450-HP engine that he called the "Air Pullman." (He had previously worked for the Pullman Company.) This was one of the most rugged planes built to date and seemed to be on the right track. In fact, it was good enough to attract the wholehearted participation of the Fords; and an improved model, the 2-AT (Air Transport-2), was put into production in a new modern factory at Dearborn. The first five planes off the line were purchased by the Ford Motor Company, which established its own private airline, transporting parts and personnel between the various Ford plants. A modern airport complete with concrete runways, terminal buildings and staff was created and led the way for future designs. All this was pretty advanced for 1924-1926! The 2-AT was the first plane to carry the FORD name in large letters on its side.

It wasn't long before Henry prodded Stout to come up with a 3-AT design that would be larger and would have three engines. This prototype had disappointing performance and a rather weird appearance. As a result, this was the last Ford plane Bill Stout designed for Ford. He was retired to the other end of the country lecturing, while a new design team was utilized, one that obviously had looked at the already famous Fokker Tri-motor, which was made of plywood and cloth. The similarity of the two designs is obvious. The Ford 4-AT (Fourth Air Transport), being made of metal, was noisier than the Fokker, but history would prove that it lasted for decades while the Fokker proved to be plagued with dry rot, separated structures, and termites. Knute Rockne was killed in a Fokker that came apart in a thunderstorm in the Midwest. The Ford 4-AT Tri-motor became a great success and it and its later and larger brother, the 5-AT with three Pratt and Whitney 450-HP Wasps, were the darlings of the emerging airline industry in the late '20s and early '30s.

In Spokane at this time, Nick Mamer had been pioneering the route between Spokane and Seattle and eastward to Minneapolis-St. Paul. This route, later referred to as the "Northern Tier," was finally lost to Northwest Airways of St. Paul when that company succeeded in obtaining the U.S. mail contract.

Nick and his embryo Mamer Air Transport Company had been flying Buhl Airsedans for several months on the route – probably because he was the Buhl dealer for the Spokane area and had sold several locally. Airlines in these early days were pretty thrilling operations! My good friend Louis Wasmer, who owned KHQ and KGA, and later KSPO and KREM, had remarked to me on several occasions how he was a passenger on a Buhl one hot afternoon in July when they took off from Butte, Montana, (elevation

5,000 plus feet). They desperately jumped the road at the end of the "airport," almost touched down unwillingly in the cemetery adjoining and, finally struggling into the air, proceeded eastward to meet Newt Wakefield, who was then flying the eastern segment from Minneapolis. Louis had been an early airplane buff in Seattle before moving to Spokane in 1925 to start radio station KHQ. He was an active sportsman pilot and aircraft owner and later backed Al Connick as a fixed base operator at Felts Field. He owned a Buhl Airsedan, then a beautiful Stinson Detroiter, followed by a Beech Stagger Wing 17, a Fairchild 24, etc. He took me with him in the Beech when I was a kid. I told him I liked the Stinson better (the *Princess Pat*, which he owned with "Daddy" Broad of Dishman), but he said, "It was too slow and just like an old maid going to a funeral, while the Stagger Wing with its retractable gear and a Jacobs 300-HP had a 200 plus MPH cruise!"

Also, Patsy Wilson (Mrs. William Harrison) and several of her school chums flew east to school once in the Buhl with memorable thrilling experiences with pilot Wakefield. Newt was the son of W. J. C. Wakefield, Spokane attorney (who served on the Old National Bank Board of Directors with August Paulsen and my grandfather in 1912). He was educated in the east and was an engineer who wanted to fly. Newt and his good friend, young Cip Paulsen, who had been backing Nick Mamer for several years, had decided to improve their pilot skills by taking advantage of the opportunity offered by the Navy Reserve. They were assigned to the training program at Sand Point Air Station in Seattle for a six-month course. Rumor

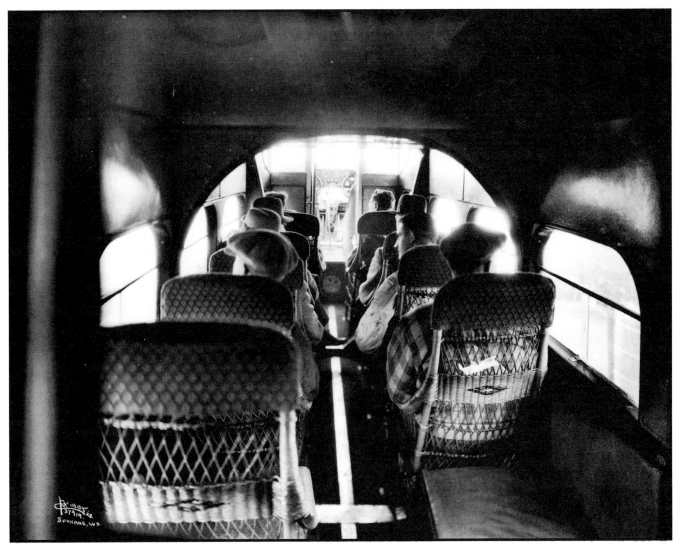

Airplane interior, Spokane Airways, Inc., November 16, 1928. *(Courtesy MAC, Libby photo L87-1.37919-28)*

has it, although I am sure it is not completely true, that this was the longest six months in the commanding officer's whole life. He was really happy to see those boys graduate!

This is understandable when you realize that the commanding officer was a friend of "Cippy's" mother, and you know that boys will be boys, especially these two! It is said (jokingly) that they spent a good deal of time at the admiral's house, eating his food, drinking his liquor, keeping him up much of the night dancing with the girls until he finally gave up and told them, "Hell, you guys stay here, I am going to move to the club to get some rest." Our heroes returned to Spokane eminently more qualified and more experienced, to pursue the challenges that happy young pilots pursue.

As a personal sidelight, I will always remember Cip as he appeared to me in 1929. I was a 12-year-old, barefaced boy just starting in outboard hydroplane racing with my new boat, *Ma's Worry I*. Some of us kids saw the big, handsome sportsman and were impressed! He had a custom-built Lincoln "boat-tail" Phaeton with an aluminum body, which was especially built for the New York Auto Show, an airplane or two, three racing boats with a truck and a driver to get them to the races, a 1,000-watt (plus) ham radio station, and a happy philosophy of life that was tough for me not to like.

After the successful 1927 National Air Races, Nick Mamer and Cip Paulsen and many others were so enthused about the future of air travel that they decided on expansion of the Mamer Air Transport. The plan was to buy a couple of Tri-motor Fords, build a new hangar to service them, and haul some passengers on the same routes they had been flying with the Buhls. The Fords cost $49,000 each, rather than the $12,500 cost of the Buhls, requiring more capital, but this investment seemed justified.

An interesting letter, on the following page, best documents the expansionary mood of the day. The letter was given to me by Charlotte Witherspoon and was written to her father, J. C. Semple, early in 1930 by Newt Wakefield, who was introducing the newly formed International Air Transport Company to prospective investors. Both the letterhead and the copy are enlightening.

The first of the three Ford Tri-motors that "lived" in Spokane in 1928-1933 had a very short life! At 10:45 a.m. on Friday, November 23, 1928, the two-week-old pride of the Spokane Airways at Felts Field dove into a potato patch on Moran Prairie about a block east of the where the KJRB transmitter facility was later located. The accident was the most violent and probably the best remembered by old-timers, because of the widespread involvement by a number of Spokane flyers. According to the headlines:

> Killed was: The chief pilot, Lt. William H. Williams, 34, (and charter member of the 116th), Louis Norman DeBurger, age 30, the ship mechanic on loan from the Ford Factory, Arthur G. Enarson, 24, business manager for the Mamer Flying Service and Kenneth Dunlap, 24, bookkeeper from Spokane. Gravely injured was D. R. Mitchell, chief mechanic of Spokane Airways who had his left foot torn off and his hip broken. Injured was Rex Heath, business manager of Spokane Airways with nose broken and possible internal injuries.

The day before, the new Ford with its happy crew and several of the Guard Squadron planes, as well as some commercial aircraft, gathered at Colfax to dedicate the new airport. The big new Tri-motor was somewhat of a novelty in this part of the country, and a number of paying passengers were hauled during the occasion. After remaining overnight, the crews were anxious to return to Spokane in the morning. They waited for the fog to lift at Colfax and when it did, about five ships took off, heading for home. When they got a few miles north of their departure point, a dense ground fog seemed to cover all of the lower terrain around Spokane.

INTERNATIONAL AIR TRANSPORT CO

DIRECTORS
A. W. Witherspoon
C. I. Paulsen
N. B. Mamer
Newton Wakefield

Subsidiary Companies
MAMER AIR TRANSPORT
MAMER FLYING SERVICE, Inc.

419-420 Paulsen Building
SPOKANE, WASHINGTON

February 20, 1930

OFFICERS
C. I. Paulsen, Pres.
N. B. Mamer, Vice-Pres.
Newton Wakefield, Vice-Pres.
L. J. Daniel, Sec-Treas.

File E 910

Mr. J. C. Semple
Allenby Apts.
Spokane, Wash.

Dear Mr. Semple:

Following the World War in 1919 Nick Mamer laid the foundation for this Company's present business when he began flying for hire, a war surplus plane, and teaching an occasional student to fly.

You, as well as everyone else in the Northwest, have witnessed the exceptional progress made by Mamer in building up step by step and developing the different branches of the Mamer Air Transport and the Mamer Flying Service which now include the only United States Government Approved School of Flying in the Pacific Northwest; Government Forest Patrol contract work, sales agencies for the Curtiss Wright line of airplanes and a general flying business.

In order to take advantage of and capitalize on Mamer's nation-wide reputation, and to develop and expand the present profitable operations of the Mamer Companies, the International Air Transport Co. has just authorized a $350,000 stock issue to provide for the establishment of an air line from Spokane to St. Paul.

The purpose of offering this issue to the public is to create ownership interest and to enlist active support and patronage by allotting a limited amount of stock to every community along the route of the Spokane-St. Paul air line.

The Northern Route is a strategic military airway and is the only major air line remaining for development in the United States today.

In a few days you will receive complete detailed information of the financial plan.

Very truly yours,

INTERNATIONAL AIR TRANSPORT CO.

By *Newton Wakefield*
Newton Wakefield
Vice President

NW:FEC

Pilot William H. Williams decided to let two of the other members of the crew fly the plane around above Spokane for a while "to see if the fog would not soon burn off." He retired to the main cabin to play cards with De Burger, Dunlap and Enarson, leaving Heath and Mitchell at the controls.

After about an hour, Lt. Williams and De Burger came forward and announced they were going to take the plane down. Because Lt. Williams had noticed several of the Guard 02-H planes plunge into the fog after circling for some time and then apparently getting through, he "felt he could make it." Actually Lt. Rose made a forced landing on Peone Prairie, Lt. Wadsworth tore off the undercarriage of his ship when he made a forced landing near Millwood, while Major Haynes, the commanding officer of the 116th after Jack Fancher, who was possibly older and wiser than his colleagues, turned back and landed at Rosalia. Also, Sergeant Forbes turned back and landed at Colfax, while Ralph Daniels of Spokane Airways turned around and landed first at Thornton and then Colfax.

Heath begged Billy not to try it and suggested they return to Colfax, but Williams, who had a reputation for being an excellent flyer, felt he could find a hole in the murk alright. Mitchell and Heath returned to the cabin and Enarson said, "Heath, I'll deal you a hand to see whether it's hell or not," and dealt the cards around. The first card up was the queen of spades! At this time, Williams asked them to "even up the cargo" (two on one side and two on the other). A few seconds later, according to the detailed report in the *Spokesman-Review* quoting the survivor Heath, "You couldn't see anything when we felt the swish of branches against the undercarriage. I saw the sun beneath and the ground flew up."

The plane hit with terrific force. It was in a sharp bank at the time of the crash, its left wing struck, tearing it off, the nose struck the ground, rebounded once, struck again, and turned over on its back. There was no fire. Due to the dense fog, no one saw the crash, but it was heard over a wide area. Several people rushed to the scene and found the conscious Heath and the others all thrown clear of the shattered wreckage of the all-metal plane. Although the police emergency ambulance had rushed to the wreck, several of the local citizens used their own cars and transported two of the injured to the police emergency room in the City Hall.

Police Chief Wesley Turner declared it was the "worst smash he had ever seen," according to the newspaper report. His description of "bits of wreckage strewn fully two blocks around the prairie and cabin chairs were all over the field, and bits of metal and parts of the motors were flung in all directions," confirms my own observations of that day.

I had gone home to lunch from the Hutton School at noon when my father rushed in from the office and said that the big Ford Tri-motor had just crashed about a mile south of our 26th Avenue home. For some reason or other, we, like many others, drove to the scene and the sight has remained with me through the many years of flying I have done since! I also picked up a small torn piece of the aluminum structure and took it home for a souvenir.

The plane was of great interest to me at age eleven, as I was in the middle of my adolescent "crush" on airplanes and flyers in general. My father's friend Lawrence Sherman, who was in the 116th Air National Guard Squadron, had talked to me about taking some dual instructions with him in Spokane Airways' trainer, an "International" biplane with OX-5 or a Hisso engine. The company had just built the long shed-type hangar south of the Guards' headquarters building and were operating a Buhl Airsedan, a Curtiss Robin, a Ryan B-1, and had just added the Ford to their then growing fleet of planes.

This 1928 photo by Charles Libby shows the first Ford 4-AT taking on a little fuel in the good old fashioned way.

Incidentally, the company was owned by Sam Wilson who was the "promoter" of the Golconda Mine in Kellogg, Idaho, and both my father and Vic Dessert, as well as many other people, purchased stock in the mine. I remember Vic kidding Dad about how crazy they must be to invest in such an obviously risky development and especially with such an enthusiastic promoter as Sam.

Another interesting sidelight to the story is the really "grand" maiden trip of the Ford from Dearborn, Michigan. Sam Wilson invited several friends to go with him on the train to bring the great "Bird" back to Spokane. According to General Hillford Wallace, Bill Williams was chosen to be chief pilot because he had a good reputation and was considered quite professional in local flying circles,

The trip took on some aspects of a maiden voyage of the *Queen Mary* in that, in addition to caviar and roast chicken, Sam brought along his favorite waiter from the Coeur d'Alene Hotel in Spokane, a friendly and well-liked pro by the name of Tom Rogers. Tom tried to make all the guests feel comfortable and secure and, as part of his contribution to the success of the trip, he made up a "ditty" (to the tune of "Casey Jones") that documented the voyage colorfully from day to day and kept the passengers' minds on happy things.

The original script on hotel stationery follows at the end of the chapter. You can visualize how Tom Rogers put this down on paper after composing the verses en route for group singing, and gave it to Mr. Wilson, as his sincere letter of appreciation and to act as a record of the historic occasion.

A little bit of the daring spirit that "pilot Billy" displayed might have faintly foreshadowed the sad event to take place only a few days in the future.

Sam Wilson was deeply shaken by the news of the crash when he was notified of it while attending a Northwest Mining Investment Company meeting in Vancouver, B. C. He did not replace the Ford and soon abandoned his aviation interest, leaving the Mamer Air Transport alone to carry on the story of Ford Tri-motors in Spokane.

Mamer's two Fords were called the *West Wind I* and the *West Wind II.* The hangar that serviced them, but was not large enough to house them, was built in 1929 just west of the 1932 Felts Field Terminal Building. (This was later owned by Wasmer and then Claude Calkins.) The airline business didn't work out very well for Mamer Air Transport. Northwest Airways, forerunner of Northwest Airlines, landed the U.S. mail contract in the Minneapolis-St. Paul area and then eventually extended west to Spokane and Seattle. The stock market crash in 1929 and the depression that followed, pretty well squashed the dreams of success for the Mamer Air Transport. Nick had proven the technical feasibility of the northern route, but found the economics unsatisfactory without a mail contract. The two Fords were mainly used on the Spokane, Yakima, Portland run, the Spokane-Seattle flight and on special charters. The Fords were finally sold, and Nick later went to work for Northwest Airlines as chief pilot on the northern tier route (more on that later).

"Pilot Billy" really wrapped this one up! (Spokane Airways Ford, 1928).

A November 24, 1928 *Spokesman-Review* article regarding the fatal Tri-motor accident.

About the last information I have on the *West Wind II* is a picture of it being loaded with "20 quarter barrels and 50 packages of Gilt Top beer" that were being shipped to Osborn (Wallace-Kellogg) Airport to satisfy the temporary thirst of the miners when the community was cut off by the unusual floods in December 1933! Finally another picture in my files shows a Ford AT-5 at Felts Field in 1935 that was being operated by United Airlines between Spokane and Pendleton, but more on that in the next chapter.

By the middle of the 1930s, most of the Fords had disappeared from first line use, being replaced by faster and more modern planes. The "Tin Goose Era" was essentially over in the United States.

Aircraft and personnel of Spokane Airways at Felts Field in 1928 before their Ford Tri-motor, from left to right, a Buhl Airsedan, a Ryan B-1, an International with OX-5, and a Curtiss Robin with OX-5. (The Curtiss Robin, color red, was displayed at the Spokane Interstate Fair in 1928.)

This 1932 Libby photo taken at Felts Field shows Nick Mamer in his new 1932 Ford V-8 Coupe, purchased from Phil Garnett, owner of Universal Auto Company. The Mamer Air Transport's Ford Tri-motors are just behind: *Westwind I* on the left and *Westwind II* on the right. The biplane in the background is the United Airline Boeing 40-B4 mail and passenger plane then in use. Also, the round-roof hangar at the left is the Bigelow Johnson headquarters, later to become home for Wallace Air Service.

The "AIRSEDAN"
Buhl Aircraft Co. Marysville, Mich.

Our whole family went up with Nick Mamer in the Buhl Airsedan in 1928. The Mamer Air Service was the Buhl dealer in Spokane. Buhl was originally a milk can manufacturer before going into the airplane business. Mamer flew Buhls in his regular commercial airline and charter work and also in the National Air Derby. The *Spokane Sun-God* was a late model Buhl Sesquiplane.

SPECIFICATIONS
Weight Empty .... 2100 lbs.
Wing Span .... 42 feet
Wing Area .... 320 sq. ft.
Length .... 28 feet
Pay Load .... 1000 lbs.
Seating Capacity--Pilot and 4 Passengers

PERFORMANCE
High Speed (sea level) .... 120 M.P.H.
Landing Speed .... 45 "
Cruising Speed .... 100 "
Service Ceiling .... 14000 feet

POWER PLANT
Wright Whirlwind J.5
Horse Power .... 200 at 1800 R.P.M.
Fuel Capacity .... 70 gals.
Oil Capacity .... 4 Gals.

EQUIPMENT
Self Starter, Brakes, Metal Propeller, Compass, Air Speed Indicator, Navigation Lights, Tachometer, Altimeter, Clock, Fire Extinguisher; Fuel, Oil Pressure and Oil Temperature Gauges; Air Corps Throttles, Strainer and Fuel Valve.

Price $12,500.   Flyaway, Our Field
BUHL AIRCRAFT CO.
Marysville, Michigan

Spokane Airways' Buhl Airsedan with Wright J-5 in 1928. It was named after Sam Wilson's Golconda Mine in Kellogg, Idaho. Mamer sold a number of these fine five-place ships in the Spokane area, 1928.

A 1932 photo showing a 1931 Auburn convertible sedan standing beside the Mamer Air Transport's *West Wind II*, powered by Wright 300 HP J-6 engines. Plane in background, with the United Airlines logo, is a Boeing 40B-4 mail plane.

Mamer Air Transport's *Westwind II* receiving a cargo of Gilt Top beer to be flown to the miners in Wallace during the flood of December 1933, when all the roads, as well as telephone wires, were washed out. *(Courtesy MAC, Libby photo L87-1.3154-33)*

A part of Felts Field in 1929. The three newly constructed commercial hangars are on the right while the Spokane Airways' hangar is the black one in the foreground. The Mamer Flying Service's old hangars are out of the picture to the left. The company's name was later changed to Mamer Air Transport. The new National Guard Operations building is the brick one on the left. Next to it is the original 1919 hangar with the FELTS FIELD sign on it. This burned soon after. The other two black hangars (one with SPOKANE AIR PORT on it) were the ones erected in 1924 by the Air National Guard Squadron.

Coeur d'Alene HOTEL

SPOKANE, WASH., U.S.A.

This Song is Respectfully Dedicated to:

PILOTS W. H. WILLIAMS AND LOUIS DeBURGER, AND TO MR. SAM J. WILSON AND PARTY ON HIS TRI-MOTOR GOOD-WILL SHIP FROM DETROIT TO SPOKANE

NOVEMBER 9th to 13th, 1928.

Tom Rogers.

- - - - - -

Tune - "Casey Jones."

1. Come all you people if you want to hear
   About a flying trip up in the air
   William Williams was the pilot's name
   On a Ford Tri-Motor ship he won his fame.
   In old Detroit he looked at his chart
   He said, Mr. Wilson before we start
   We may have snow and we may have rain
   And we may have caskets made in old Spokane.

   ### Chorus

   Pilot Bill, mounted to the cockpit
   Pilot Bill, map in his hand
   Pilot Bill, mounted to the cockpit
   Flying from Detroit back to old Spokane.

2. In old Wisconsin when things looked blue
   The snow was blowing when he tried to go thru
   He said to DeBurger, what shall we do
   I think we better set her down in Baraboo.
   Early next morning after taking the air
   We sailed over Menominee and old Eau Claire
   He shut off the motors, we began to fall
   But he made a perfect landing in old St. Paul.

   Chorus.

3. We left St. Paul that very same day
   For Omaha bound, three hundred miles away
   I said, Mr. Wilson, just take a look
   For he's going to put her down in old Ft. Crook.
   Early next morning, hear the motors sing
   We're going to take the air now for old Rock Spring
   Warm her up, boys, there's no time to waste
   Said Pilot Bill Williams with a smile on his face.

   Chorus.

Coeur d'Alene HOTEL

SPOKANE, WASH., U.S.A.

4. We left Rock Springs for Salt Lake bound
   With coyotes running all over the ground
   With a tail wind blowing and clouds were low
   When we thought we saw Ogden but 'twas Pocatello.
   Said Pilot Bill and DeBurger too
   Gas her up quick 'cause we want to go thru
   I felt sorry for the gas pump man
   'Cause he had to pump a hundred fifty gallon by hand.

   Chorus.

5. We left Pocatello 'bout a quarter to three
   Headed right straight for old Boise
   Everybody feeling mighty spic and span
   'Cause we're getting mighty close to sunny old Spokane.
   In Boise folks tried with all their might
   To keep our old ship there for the night
   The weather man said, You will hit a storm
   But another little storm couldn't do us any harm.

   Chorus.

6. Up in the mountains with the sun gone down
   Over clouds like cotton, we couldn't see the ground
   Everybody quiet, some were feeling blue
   But the old tri-motors all were hitting true.
   Ten thousand feet up in the dark
   A light on the ground looked like a spark
   Pilot Bill said to nose her down
   Everybody felt better, it was Lewis Town..

   Chorus.

7. Just look to your left, just look to your right
   For miles and miles see the beautiful sight
   Now we're flying over old Spokane
   Feeling mighty happy, want to go again.
   To Pilot Bill and DeBurger too
   Mr. Sam J. Wilson, here's to you,
   To the best old tri-motor ship that is
   Mr. Ellsworth French says - He--re tiz.

   Final Chorus.

   Pilot Bill, sitting in the cockpit,
   Pilot Bill, DeBurger at his side,
   Pilot Bill, sitting in the cockpit,
   Thank you, Mr. Wilson, for this wonderful ride.

   --Tom Rogers.

Chapter VII

The Spokane Sun-God

The *Spokane Sun-God* before the famous endurance flight with seven barrels of Texaco gasoline (350-plus gallons) and 20 gallons of Texaco lubricating oil, all of which was put aboard. The plane was the latest model Buhl "Sesquiplane" (with pointed lower stub wings) loaned by the factory and equipped with the new 300 HP Wright J-6 engine. Art Walker, Nick Mamer, and the Texaco representative Jack Allenberg are in the foreground with the Spokane Airways hangar on the left and the Parkwater School on the right.

The second major successful event that brought national (and world) attention to Spokane was the flight of the *Spokane Sun-God* in the late summer of 1929. This flight by Nick Mamer and his young associate, Art Walker, was also sponsored by the National Air Derby Association in cooperation with the Buhl Aircraft Company and Texaco. The local committee this time was much the same as in 1927, with Vic Dessert, chairman, Charles Hebberd, Leon Boyle, Ellsworth French, Nick Pierong, Chuck Adams, Capt. Wadsworth, Major Haynes, William Cowles Jr., Harry Goetz, Bob Owen and Jack Allenberg.

The plan was to fly nonstop from Spokane to San Francisco to New York and return, refueling in flight from other aircraft. Three planes were regularly used in the *Sun-God* flight: the *Sun-God* itself, which was a new Buhl Sedan made available by the factory, another Buhl serving as a refueling plane with Bob

Oscar Levitch and Nick Mamer in front of plane, August 13, 1929. *(Courtesy MAC, Libby collection, L87-140128-29)*

Wilson at the stick and Neal O'Connell as the hose man, and a Ryan B-1 also serving as a refueling plane with Verne Brookwalter as pilot and Al Coppula as hose man. By a prearranged schedule, they met Mamer at designated points along the way and successfully refueled the *Sun-God* in mid-air.

The line of flight was from Spokane to Portland, Eugene, Medford, Oakland, Reno, Salt Lake City, Rock Springs, Cheyenne, North Omaha, Des Moines, Cedar Rapids, Chicago, Cleveland, and New York, then back to Cleveland, Chicago, Madison, St. Paul and west to Spokane.

In the late afternoon of August 15, 1929, Nick and Art took to the air (800 lbs. over-weight) at Felts Field and began their historic trip. Things went more or less according to plan until they came to Rock Springs, Wyoming, where the rough air caused a near-fatal mishap when the *Sun-God's* propeller cut the refueling hose hanging down from the refueling plane. Aviation gasoline is especially volatile and a very great hazard existed as the fuel sprayed down on and all over the helpless *Sun-God*. Fortunately, it did not burst into flames.

The cutting of the only available hose, and the by-then very low tanks of the *Sun-God* almost ended the flight, but the team put together an effort with the remaining 20 feet of hose and successfully refueled at night with the aid of a flashlight tied to the end.

They proceeded eastward through heavy rain and a lightning storm over Pennsylvania and refueled over New York with a "borrowed" crew they had never seen before. At Cleveland on the way back they refueled with another crew in full sight of the people attending the 1929 National Air Races, then winged their way westward to meet their regular refueling planes.

Mamer's *Spokane Sun-God*.

Nick Mamer and Indians in ceremonial dress at the christening of the *Spokane Sun-God* **airplane on August 15, 1929.** *(Courtesy MAC. Libby photo L87-1.40153-29)*

Over Aberdeen, South Dakota, a 50 mph howling wind didn't make the transfer any easier! Over Miles City, Montana, at midnight, the fuel running low, the endurance fliers dropped a message at the airport asking for an emergency refueling. Frank Wiley, a commercial pilot, came up at dawn and lowered gasoline in a five-gallon milk can that swung and swayed at the end of a rope. Time after time, Wiley brought up the milk can of fuel. The can bumped and battered the *Sun-God* fuselage each time contact was made, but the flight went on.

Closer to home, smoke from forest fires hampered navigation over Montana:

> Forty-nine times the *Sun-God* received new supplies of gas and oil and its crew's food supply was replenished. Seven different refueling crews, only two of which Mamer had ever worked with before, risked their necks to keep the *Sun-God* flying. When the plane took off in Spokane it had on board a gallon of water, three quarts of coffee, whole wheat bread, meat sandwiches, cheese and meat sandwich spread, a dozen oranges and a jar of pickles! An extra 200 gallon gasoline tank in the fuselage created some problems for the crew. It left room for one man only at the controls. The flyers could not stand erect and there was no place for them to walk.
>
> In the tail of the plane was a small mattress but Mamer said it was never used for sleeping. It was usually covered with oil cans, food containers and other equipment. Mamer said he and Walker had no sleep during the five days and nights.
>
> When they weren't busy flying and refueling one or the other had to spend exhausting hours transferring gasoline from the fuselage tank into the wing tanks with the hand device called a wobble pump.

A Texaco plane refueling the *Sun-God* in Flight.

One of the most amazing aspects of the flight was that in 1929 the *Sun-God* did not have the capability of using a two-way radio. All arrangements had to be made in advance by telegram and letters, and all communications from the crew to ground and vice versa were handled by notes written on paper. Nick took along some little weights to help drop hastily written notes with requests for supplies and services.

Nick acted as a correspondent for the *Spokesman-Review* and the North American Newspaper Alliance during the flight, writing his stories in the air and dropping them over airports as they flew. Attempts at new endurance records were popular and common in those times, since the Army Air Corps *Question Mark*, a Tri-motor Fokker, had remained aloft for 151 hours, refueled by its single Douglas 02-H observation plane over Southern California skies in January 1929. The *Question Mark's* crew of five, incidentally, included Lt. Elwood Quesada, Capt. Ira Eaker, and Major Tooey Spaatz, all well known in World War II.

When the *Sun-God* arrived safely over Spokane about noon on August 20th, five days after departing, Nick dropped several notes to his ground crews. Nick and Art did not attempt to land, as they needed further instructions. Nick advised that they were both in pretty good shape and could continue on around the circuit again, or just stay in the air around the Northwest, thereby piling up more hours toward the record.

One of the notes was addressed to Vic Dessert, the chairman of the committee, and was marked confidential. It read as follows:

I want to let you know the situation. One magneto on the engine is out. It has been out for some time but we have kept quiet about it. It means if we lose one plug on the good one, we are down. There is no way we can get to it to repair it. I want you to call a conference and explain the situation. I would prefer not to have anything mentioned to the public because the Wright Company has been so interested.

The 300-HP Wright engine on the *Sun-God* was a new model and an improvement over the 220-HP one that Lindbergh used two years before. Nick was proud of its performance and did not want to reflect poorly on it in any way. Wright officials had helped him on the way and at Roosevelt Field, over New York, an official of the company had sent a note up to them. Nick's message to the committee continued:

You know the magnetos are merely accessories and this motor has been so sweet. In view of this condition, it would be extremely inadvisable to attempt another transcontinental flight, unless this trouble were remedied. I am feeling OK., although I know Art is just a little tired. However, we are eager to remain up as we are over the peak and nothing worries us anymore. You know the first 100 are always the toughest.

With this condition of the engine, it would be hopeless to attempt to break the endurance record [of the *Question Mark*], although we feel we should make a trip to the coast and anywhere else that would not involve night flying over hazardous country. In the meantime, you could get set for our landing and the committee could announce the results we have accomplished and invite me to land or any way you see fit. In the meantime, we will hang on, awaiting developments. It is safe enough over the airport as we can always land safely, and it would also be quite safe anywhere, even with the magneto out during daylight. But you know what it would mean at night. Nick

P.S. The special oiling system for the rockers is out on three cylinders – Not serious.

The *Spokane Sun-God* first team! On the left, hose man Neal O'Connell and pilot Bob Wilson who handled the Buhl refueling plane. Art Walker and Nick Mamer are in the center. On the right are pilot Alphonse "Al" Coppula and hose man Verne Brookwalter, who flew the Ryan B-1 special refueling plane.

There was a hurried conference on the ground, after which Mr. Dessert sent up the following note at 2:25 p.m. to the *Sun-God* crew.

> It is the unanimous action of the trustees of the National Air Derby Association that you be directed to land at 6 o'clock tonight. Wakefield will be up with supplies as you ordered at 3 o'clock. If refueling plane arrives, will start refueling demonstration at 5 o'clock. We are publicly announcing that you will land at 6 o'clock.

The next note from Nick advised:

> The magneto picked up again and is hitting. I found that by retarding its spark, it picked up. It must be shorted when the throttle is all advanced. OK with us to remain up indefinitely. We would at least like to go to the coast and back. Whatever you say is OK. How about it?   Nick

Still another message read:

> If you will send up some paper and pencils and indicate who you want me to write to, I will get busy, now that we can rest around the field. If we stay up, we want a complete change of all clothes, soap and water – hot water to wash. Mrs. Mamer will get these. We feel like we have just bathed in hot oil – dirty as hell but happy.   Nick

Nick Mamer inside the *Sun-God*. Note the large tank ahead of the panel.

Art Walker (left) and Nick Mamer, pilots of the *Spokane Sun-God* on its nonstop trip across the continent and back. *(Photo courtesy MAC, Libby photo L87-1.40119-29.)*

Food supplies were sent aloft and were lowered to the flyers in cans at the end of long ropes. Mamer dropped the following note: "The ship is just plumb full of food and thermos bottles. Please don't send up any more tonight. When making the next contact, lower down rope with weights on the end. We have a ton of stuff to send back. Nick"

Mamer and Walker remained in the air nearly six hours after coming over Felts Field. Refueling caused them trouble and exasperation, as the following notes dropped by Mamer indicate:

> What a fine reception we get! You send that bird up in the Buhl "Sesqui" and he does not realize that I cannot look into the glaring sun and see his ship also. Then after two hours, he finally realizes what is wrong and the man who is lowering the bag is scared and does not know what to do. You can see why it is impossible to keep a schedule. There are not enough pilots with this experience. Another mistake they make: when they see you coming for them, they start going like hell, making it all more difficult. Send up Wilson and Cop [Coppula].   Nick

The newspaper account of the event points out that this was an emergency refueling crew. They were trying to lower gasoline in tin cans at the end of ropes, as they could not operate a hose and were not so equipped. Mamer's two trained refueling crews were not available. The *Sun-God* crew finally cut the tops off and filled the tank from the open cans.

It was also reported that nerves were on edge after the strain of five days and nights in the air. The bungling of the refueling over Felts Field taxed Mamer's usually good nature to the breaking point and he dropped a stinging note to the pilot of the refueling plane as follows: "How in the hell do you expect us to see you when you fly into the sun?"

To the men on the ground, he wrote in some exasperation: "You have got to use your bean on messages. You can say anything. It will be OK with us. Between flying, writing, pumping gas and cussing the refueling crews for being slow, flying is simple compared with this writing."

Also it was recorded that some of the notes Nick dropped that afternoon were stained with some blood. While working on the engine, he had cut his arm and when six o'clock rolled around, he and Art were undoubtedly very happy to land at Felts Field and complete the flight successfully.

Although the flight did not break the world's endurance record of the Army Tri-motored Fokker *Question Mark*, it did set the following records and achievements:

1. World's record nonstop mileage (7,200-plus miles)
2. First transcontinental refueling flight
2. First night refueling
3. First refueling at an altitude above 8,000 feet
4. Staying aloft five days and nights under severe handicap

A telegram from the White House signed by President Herbert Hoover partially illustrates the impact the feat generated: "Congratulations on the successful completion of your nonstop refueling flight across the continent and return. It is a further demonstration of the ever-widening scope of the practical utility of aircraft."

The *Sun-God* was in the air 120 hours, one minute and 40 seconds, and covered 7,200 miles. This far exceeded the 4,663 miles flown by the Italian aviators Ferranian and De Prete from Rome to Natal, Brazil, and the nonstop mileage of the Graf Zepplin from Friedrichshafen, Germany, to Tokyo, Japan, of 6,880 miles.

The crowd started to gather for the landing of the *Spokane Sun-God* at 2:00 p.m. although the plane did not touch down until between 5:00 and 6:00 p.m. *(Washington Air National Guard photo)*

A special sealed barograph had been installed by Valentine Gephart of Seattle who was then the secretary of the National Aeronautics Association. This device would prove the aircraft did not touch down anywhere before the end of its grueling journey.

In August 1979, I had the privilege to attend the celebration of the 50th anniversary of the flight in the Aerospace Museum in Seattle. Art Walker was the person honored, and master of ceremonies was Ernie Gann. Gretchen Boeing was in charge of the arrangements, and a wonderful time was had by all.

I was impressed with the way Art Walker had held his youthfulness. He was still handsome, trim and very much alive. His children and grandchildren were there to share his numerous acclaims and awards. (Art had been an airline and corporate pilot and then director of aviation for Standard Oil Company.) One of the tributes that impressed me most was from the Chief of Staff in Washington, who pointed out that what the flight of the *Sun-God* had been first to do (using in-flight refueling to extend range) had been the basis for all the S.A.C. operations since its inception, thereby allowing it to fulfill its mission of deterrent force in the preservation of peace in our world. One way of looking at it – it all started in Spokane, Washington!

The *Spokane Sun-God* and the Buhl refueling plane transfer supplies over the Spokane Valley at 2:30 p.m. on August 18, 1929. (*Washington Air National Guard photo*)

THE ARCTIC PATROL, January 1930

As a result of Spokane's 1927 National Air Races and the 1929 *Sun-God* endurance flight, Spokane was in the national limelight. The Army Air Corps took notice and selected Spokane for a winter training exercise. During January of 1930, the Selfridge Field, Michigan Pursuit Squadron decided to hold a special training exercise. The plan was to see how this first-line organization of the Army Air Corps could react to a mission that would require them to move into battle in the peak of winter in this northern clime. Sixteen Curtiss "Hawk" (P-1) pursuit planes, as they were called (later designated fighters), were readied for the trip. The planes were equipped with skis rather than their normal wheels and the destination was none other than Spokane, Washington. The "Hawks" were accompanied by a tri-motored support aircraft in this cold cross-country deployment. The support plane carried the squadron's mechanics, spare parts and other necessary equipment to keep the unit operational en route and in the field. Spokane was excited, and waiting patiently.

There was at least one major problem as I recall the occasion: There wasn't any snow at Felts Field! The weather was clear and cold and the meteorologist couldn't see any snow in the immediate future for Spokane. As the Squadron, which was by this time specially named the "Arctic Patrol" and referred to as the "Arctic Flyers," was anxious to depart Michigan, the 116th Squadron in Spokane suggested landing on the ice at Liberty Lake or Newman Lake rather than at their snowless headquarters at Felts Field. This was okay with the Arctic Patrol boys, but they stated they would like to have about ten inches of ice, if possible, to be safe. Reports from the local lakes only showed four to six inches, and during the time the planes were battling their way westward through snow-covered North Dakota and Montana, the papers made much news about the ice conditions on the lakes. Cold weather helped and Newman Lake was chosen as the destination. After all, the Arctic Flyers would find it more like the real thing if they had to set up base on an isolated frozen lake. In spite of numerous harrowing experiences winging toward Spokane, at least 12 fighters of the group finally completed the journey.

On the weekend, our family drove out to Newman Lake in our 1929 La Salle Cadillac sedan and looked things over. We drove onto the ice at Honeymoon Bay and nervously proceeded around the point to the next bay where some of the planes were parked. I remember the uncertain feeling I had about driving on the ice in the car, but reasoned that if it would support the planes and the other cars, it would probably hold us!

It was said that the flight taught the military a great deal about winter flying and operation in the field. After several days, the Arctic Flyers returned to their home base in Michigan, older but wiser. (Several years later in 1935-1936 the Selfridge Field Squadron was equipped with the then-new Boeing P-26 aircraft which was the production version of the XP-936 low-wing fixed-gear radial engine pursuit plane, famous for ground looping and nose-over shenanigans unbecoming to the Boeing breed.)

The above and preceding photos are from the Selfridge, Michigan, Field Pursuit Squadron Curtiss Hawks, equipped with skis at Honeymoon Bay on Newman Lake in 1930. *(Courtesy MAC, Libby photo L87-1.41389-30)*

Chapter VIII

The Airlines Cometh, Thank Heavens

Fashionable lady giving mail to Varney/United Airlines in 1932. *(Courtesy MAC, Libby photo L87-1.1561-32)*

We have already learned how the early post-World War I aviation companies visualized and planned the coming of air transportation to Spokane. First, the 1919 dream of the Northwest Aviation Company to jump into daily flights from Spokane to Tacoma, then Spokane to Seattle, and finally to the east was pretty advanced for their day! No airline, or for that matter even the word, existed at that time, but many could see that the wartime development of the airplane was, sooner or later, going to change the nature of the transportation patterns in the United States and the world.

Second, by the late twenties, Nick Mamer had proven, pretty much to his own satisfaction at least, that the northern route to St. Paul was technically feasible and desirable. He had flown it with passengers in the Buhl during the summer months and had hoped to get a mail contract to help economically. Northwest Airways of St. Paul was started in 1926 and flew airmail between the Twin Cities and Chicago. Army pilots had flown the same route for nine months, but after losing eight airplanes and four pilots, discontinued the service on June 30, 1921.

By 1926, with the passing of the Air Commerce Act and the creation of the Aeronautics Branch of the Department of Commerce, the Post Office Department turned over the flying of the airmail to commercial operators on a contract basis. Northwest Airways was the successful bidder on Airmail Route #9. By 1927 they started to haul a few passengers as well and, by the end of 1928, extended to Milwaukee and Green Bay. The company went through a corporate reorganization and expanded in 1929, and was among the first to uniform their flight crews. During 1930, Northwest enjoyed tremendous growth in the Minnesota, Wisconsin and Illinois area. By 1931 Northwest Airways officials began casting about for new routes to the west.

Meanwhile, back in Spokane, the Chamber of Commerce renewed the effort to promote a northern air mail route from Chicago directly west to Spokane and Seattle. J. C. Ralston, a Spokane engineer, prepared an air map of the United States. According to James Ford of the Chamber, "He made studies showing terrain, distances, and other information necessary for air travel. He showed that the Northern route was the shortest transcontinental route and that maximum altitudes were much less than on the Central route." Cooperation in the campaign was secured from the Seattle, Minneapolis, and St. Paul chambers of commerce, and the effort to promote the northern route continued.

The author's version of the Varney Airlines Stearman, drawn at age 12, 1929. He won a prize of one dollar from the Spokane Daily Chronicle in the "Hyas Tilikum" contest for this drawing.

U.S. airmail being transported by Northwest Airlines Inc. from Felts Field. *(Courtesy MAC, Forde-Leiser photographers, Mamer-Shreck Collection L84-256.45,)*

Airmail pilot Russ Owen poses with his new DeSoto Roadster in 1929. The plane is the Varney Airline Stearman used first in the Pasco-Spokane leg. Later the Boeing 40B-4 was utilized after Varney became part of United Airlines.

To the south things started to look up also. Walter T. Varney, who owned the Varney Speed Lines, was the successful bidder on a segment of the route that ran from Pasco to Elko, Nevada, and on to Salt Lake City. On April 6, 1926, Leon D. Cuddeback departed to Pasco at 6:23 a.m. in the Varney Airlines Swallow aircraft and headed southeast. This turned out to be the very humble beginning of what was later to become United Airlines. Spokane was envious of Pasco, and a drive was started to induce Varney to extend to Spokane. The Chamber mounted a big publicity campaign to get our citizens airmail conscious. A pilot and plane were hired to survey the route. Then in 1928, Felix Warren, a pioneer stagecoach driver, was commissioned to haul a "big bunch" of airmail to Pasco in an old Thorobrace Stagecoach to be loaded on the plane. Airmail stamps had been sold to practically every Spokane businessman. Varney and the Post Office Department were convinced, and by 1929 the new airline, which by then was successfully operating from Salt Lake City to Portland and up to Seattle, added the Pasco-Spokane service. Spokane finally had the much-desired direct connection to the national airmail system.

To celebrate the happy occasion, the Spokane group had a large number of wood "postcards" made from ponderosa pine cut in the McGoldrick Mill and re-manufactured by the White Pine Sash Co., whose owner, Henry Klopp, was a good friend of my grandfather's. The idea was to generate some airmail traffic for the first flight, to commemorate the day and to bring greetings from Spokane. The wood postcard in my collection was given to me on the 50th anniversary of the flight by a longtime and valued employee of our company, Eric H. Anderson. I remember him when I was a young man working at the mill. He was a cherished and shining example of the old school of professional lumber workers. A scan of the pine wood card is displayed directly below:

A scan of the Ponderosa pine wood postcard from Eric Anderson.

Eric's comments attached to the memento are as follows:

On September 15, 1929 at 5:40 p.m. two planes left Felts Field for Pasco, one to continue to Portland and the other to Salt Lake City. More than 5,000 persons were at the airport to see the take-off which marked the first airmail service out

Relics such as these were rather numerous in the past.

of Spokane. One of the first planes was piloted by Russ Owens, the other by L. D. Cuddeback. Exactly one year later passenger service to Chicago started (via Pasco) with planes leaving Spokane at 5:40 p.m. and arriving the next evening at 6 o'clock. The ship carried four passengers and during the 25-hour flight they had to be content with a snack served at airports when they stopped en route.

The way I remember it was that at first they hauled mail only once a day (in-out) in a Stearman "Mail Wing." This must be true because I won a prize of one dollar from the *Spokane Daily Chronicle* in the "Hyas Tilikum" contest with my very poor drawing of the plane complete with the Varney Airlines logo.

Later, as Eric Anderson has stated, Varney (United) put on the big Boeing biplane, Model 40-B4, which had a 550-horsepower Pratt & Whitney engine, an enclosed cabin for four passengers in the middle, as well as the mail compartment and the pilot outside, which was the practice in those days. As our house seemed to be right on the route, I became accustomed to hearing the big plane coming in each morning and departing each evening.

In 1931 United Airlines was formed by a consolidation of several lines, including Varney and the Boeing Air Transport. (President Roosevelt busted up the "horizontal/vertical conglomerate" known as United Aircraft, which consisted of the Boeing Airplane Co., Boeing Air Transport Co., Pratt & Whitney, Hamilton Steel Propeller Co. and Chance-Vought Aircraft Co.) By 1932 the 40-B4s that came in from Pasco had the United Airlines insignia on the side. It wasn't long before the new ten-passenger Boeing low-wing, all metal, twin-engine, retractable gear 247 transport was put on the Spokane run. What a beautiful plane it was – a real forerunner of what was to come!

In the ceremony that marked the beginning of the new modern passenger service, the airline invited Governor Clarence Martin (from Cheney) and several of the Spokane business leaders to take a short local flight in the new plane. My father was one of these men and, in a typical gesture for him, he insisted that I go in his place. (This he said was appropriate as I was the third-generation representative of the largest industrial plant in the Spokane area.) Naturally I was pleased and very grateful for the privilege. It is interesting to comment here that United operated the 247 equipment into Spokane for many years. Believe it or not, in 1941 when my pilot wife and I were traveling south for a visit, with our first daughter Molly as an infant, we were passengers aboard a United Airlines 247 when it had an engine-out problem just north of Pendleton, which had replaced Pasco by this time. After a successful single-engine landing there, and with the aircraft unable to taxi up to the terminal with one fan, we walked to the building and awaited another 247 to be flown in from Portland to continue the flight.

The Felts Field Administration/Terminal Building had been built in 1932, and United occupied the east part of the main level. (Later when Northwest arrived, they were housed in the west side.) No hangar at the field was large enough to hold a multi-engine aircraft for maintenance or storage, and mechanics had to fight the bad weather outside to perform their duties.

Turning our attention east again, Northwest Airways by then had extended west to Fargo, then on to Billings, which became a major station for them. Finally, in 1933, they reached Spokane and a year later, continued on to Seattle.

For the flight from St. Paul to Spokane over the Rocky Mountains, Northwest had Lockheed design and build a fast single-engine plane called the Orion. This five-passenger "hot rod" could cruise well over 200 mph, had its pilot on the "outside" (up front) and could carry several hundred pounds of mail. The trip took 13 hours one way. When, in May 1934, the Spokane to Seattle run was established with Nick Mamer now in the Northwest first officer's seat, the popular and older Hamilton six-place (plus two pilots) single-engine "metal plane" was utilized west of Spokane.

Both of these ships were soon to be replaced by Lockheed's new modern twin transport, the advanced new Electra 10-place airliner. The demise of the single-engine airline type planes was hastened by new government rules that required all airliners to be multi-engine.

It was at this time, 1934, that Nick Mamer sold the last of his two Ford Tri-motors to a Los Angeles firm and, while delayed there, was reportedly "inspecting the new Lockheed Electra 10-place plane under construction for Northwest Airways, Inc." In February 1934, President Roosevelt, who had been feuding with the airlines, announced that all airmail contracts would be cancelled at midnight, February 19th. During the chaotic few months that followed, the Army was again called on to fly the airmail. Unfortunately, ten pilots were killed in a three-weeks period and the President was prompt to acknowledge that flying the airmail was quite a different specialty from military flying and that military equipment was different.

Also, it was in the spring of 1934 that Northwest Airways, Inc. became Northwest Airlines, Inc. and during the summer took delivery of its first Lockheed 10-A, which was put on the Twin Cities to Seattle

A United Airlines Boeing 247 over Felts Field in the mid-thirties. About five years later, a new concrete runway was put in by the military.

The Spokane Airport terminal building at Felts Field was constructed in 1932, serving 137 cities. It is now on the National Historic Register. *(Photo courtesy the Jerome Peltier Collection)*

run, retiring the speedy single-engine Orions and old Hamiltons. After the airmail contract squabble was settled and new contracts were let at a substantial savings to the taxpayer, United started serving Spokane (through Pasco) with the new 247s. The plane arrived with the mail from the south at 7:00 a.m. and, rather than sit on the ground until the 10 p.m. mail departure, flew over to Seattle with passengers and returned in the late afternoon, ready for the night mail flight again. Thus, at this time, United did compete with Northwest in the Spokane to Seattle market. They also initiated a Wenatchee stop.

Spokane now had the good fortune to be served by two leading airlines, both flying the best equipment. This was too much for Mamer Air Transport. A few months before, Northwest Airlines made a deal with Nick Mamer, and he became "Western Operations Manager" as well as chief pilot on the Twin Cities to Seattle route that he knew so well. As a result, he and Cip Paulsen had sold the Fords and then sold the Mamer (Paulsen) hangar to Louis Wasmer, who needed it to store his own plane and set up Al Connick as a fixed base operator there.

The new National Guard brick hangar, built with Civil Works Administration funds, was complete by this time, but all was not well with the airline facilities at Felts. The big new transports had to sit outside, and service on them in bad weather was painful. In developing plans for a new hangar which was to be occupied jointly by Northwest and United, a big argument began. Almost everybody spoke their piece on the subject. Wasmer said they shouldn't even build a hangar, but should continue to rent his hangar. He claimed that: "It was good enough when the rent was $30.00 per month, but when he raised it, they had the place condemned." Northwest countered: "Because of inadequate facility they had moved their shop equipment and men to Seattle." They had just spent $1,000,000 on new airplanes and could not afford to

A Guard shot of the activity at Felts Field on August 14, 1938, during a visit of the 7th Bomb Group. Note the NWA hangar, the passenger terminal and the lack of a paved runway, also how the west end of the field had been pushed back to parallel the railroad and the old Mamer hangars removed.

build, but would like to rent if the city would build the facility. The city replied that it "didn't have any interest in becoming a landlord and didn't have the money either." Finally, a plan was developed whereby Northwest Airlines would buy all the materials, the Works Progress Administration would furnish the labor, and the City of Spokane the land. The project got started, Northwest moved its maintenance people back to Spokane, they agreed to furnish United with their needs, and the fine new facility, just east of the terminal and more in keeping with the needs, was operational.

By 1936 the completion of the airway's rotating beacon lights, the necessary emergency landing fields and the new four-course A-N radio ranges along the northern route made it possible for safer nighttime schedules, and the United States Airlines System became of age. In the government regulation that followed, Northwest Airlines was given the exclusive rights on the northern route while United was compelled to serve Spokane only as an extension from Pendleton, Oregon.

In 1937 Northwest Airlines ordered a fleet of new Lockheed 14 transports. The model 10-A Electras were so successful that a new, more powerful and larger plane was needed to keep up with the demand and the competition. The new plane was known as the Zephyr (model 14-H). It was powered with twin 850-HP Pratt & Whitney Hornets, was the first to have the new Fowler flaps and carried twelve passengers plus a crew of two at over 225 mph. (Interesting to note, in 1938, Howard Hughes set a new world's record in a Zephyr, flying around the world in three days, 19 hours and 14 minutes. Also, the Zephyr became the Hudson Bomber early in World War II for the British.)

Northwest Airlines passenger airplane (Douglas) at Felts Field, June 9, 1939. *(Courtesy MAC, Libby photo L87-1.16141-39)*

Now the bad news! On January 10, 1938, Captain Mamer, co-pilot Fred West and eight of their passengers were killed in a crash of Northwest Airlines Lockheed 14-H (NC-17388) near Bozeman, Montana. The accident was a freak thing. We studied about it when I was at the University of Washington in the aeronautical engineering class. It seems all mechanical structures have a natural resonance or period of vibration. In the case of an aircraft (or aircraft sub-assembly), this vibration or "flutter" can get started in turbulence and at certain air speeds become high enough in amplitude to do structural damage. In Mamer's case the rudders began to whip like a flag in the wind. The vibration got started and reinforced itself to the point where the vertical stabilizers were separated from the tail section due to rudder flutter. Later, the cure for this was to simply add a few ounces of lead a couple of inches ahead of the hinge point of the rudders, thus placing the center of gravity of the rudder forward of the support and also changing the natural period of mechanical vibration. That's all they had to do to correct the extremely occasional problem.

THE MAMER MEMORIAL CLOCK

Spokane and the entire aviation community were shocked and deeply saddened by the death of Nick Mamer. Like Jack Fancher before him, Nick had become a very well respected and popular (adopted) favorite son. In order that future generations should have some reminder of the flyer who was truly the father of aviation in the Northwest, Spokane decided to build a Memorial Clock Tower at Felts Field to "Perpetuate the memory of N. B. Mamer."

The Mamer Memorial Clock.

The Mamer Memorial Association was formed with Governor Clarence Martin as honorary chairman and the usual faithful on the active committee. Money was raised by awarding "lifetime memberships in the association" for a small contribution. Membership cards were issued, which allowed a very broad base of the general public to be a part of the worthy project. The four-sided concrete structure was erected in the grassy area just west of the Terminal Building for all to see.

The dedication ceremony was held on May 30, 1939. The *Spokane Daily Chronicle*, in a feature story by Ellsworth C. French, who was also the information officer for the 116th Observation Squadron, ably described the event:

> Spokane placed a shrine in the lives of Mrs. Fay (Nick) Mamer and daughter, Patricia, today, and Mrs. Mamer called it a "Lasting shrine of the kind Nick would like," as the Mamer Memorial Clock was dedicated at 1:45 o'clock at Felts Field. Thousands of people packed the somewhat limited area surrounding the memorial. "Everything is just as Nick would want it, because he dearly loved Spokane, his countless friends here and Felts Field," Mrs. Mamer was quoted as saying. Governor Clarence D. Martin was present and seemed to reflect the attitude of the crowd when he said, "I flew with Nick very often and I never felt safer on the ground than I did with Nick Mamer in the air."

The ceremony was given a military dignity and impressiveness from the very first when the color company of the 161st National Guard Infantry regiment escorted Governor Martin and his party from the 41st Division headquarters to the platform and planes of the 116th Observation Squadron maneuvered in low flying formation overhead. Attorney Edward W. Robertson was master of ceremonies and Major Henry Van Winkle, chaplain of the 161st Infantry, offered a prayer. Comments by R. L. Rutter, president of the Mamer Memorial Association, were brief as he referred to the untimely death of the Northwest's number one aviator and added, "To have headed the Mamer Memorial Association has been the greatest pleasure of my life."

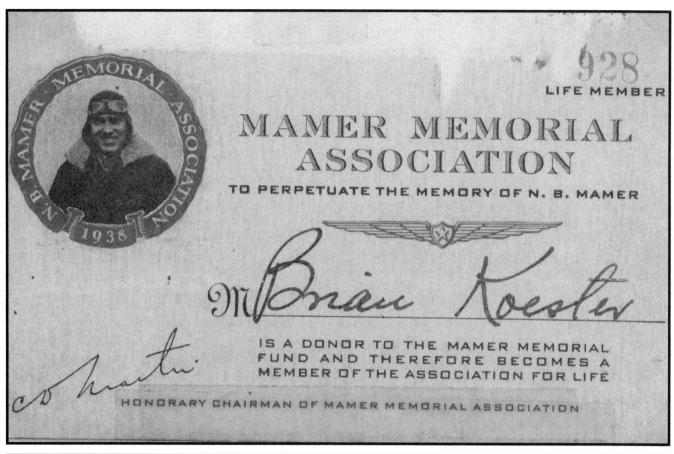

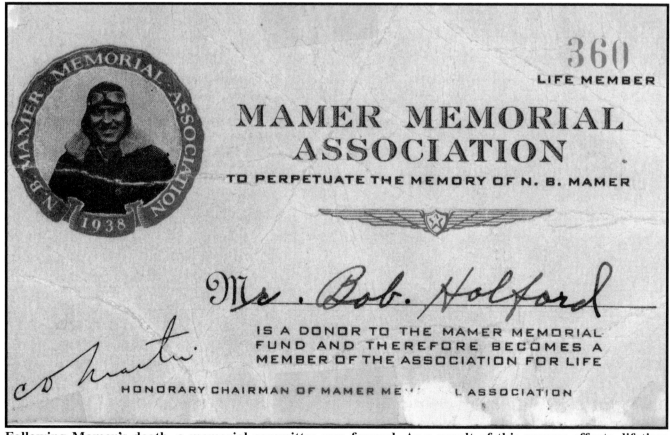

Following Mamer's death, a memorial committee was formed. As a result of this groups efforts, lifetime Mamer memorial association membership cards issued to all who financially donated to Mamer's memorial.

Major Hillford R. Wallace, commander of the 116th Observation Squadron, in which Nick Mamer was a first lieutenant, told how Nicholas Bernard Mamer, born in Minnesota on January 28, 1898, served with the Seventh Aerial Squadron, first combat squad detailed in Panama Canal Zone during the World War, later joining the Squadron here. "His splendid record as a flyer will always remain before us – an invisible beacon light, flashing outward toward the ever expanding field of aviation, and of which our brother officer was so definitely a part." Major Wallace then swung sharply to a right-hand salute, and said, "Lieutenant Mamer, we of the military salute you."

Governor Martin, in his remarks, commented:

> In the simple, but artistic concrete memorial, faced on all four sides with sweeping black hands of an electric-driven clock, I can see the life of Mr. Mamer. No finer site could have been selected than Felts Field, the home port of Nick Mamer. No finer design could have been chosen, because its artistic simplicity typifies correctly the life of our beloved friend. Nick Mamer made the supreme sacrifice to the cause of aviation. But it was not his sacrifice alone, for we have with us today his widow, Fay Mamer, and his daughter, Patricia. They are carrying on bravely where he left off. May they always find peace and happiness in this tribute to the memory of one whom they loved. To you, Mrs. Mamer, and to you, Patricia, and in behalf of the Mamer Memorial Association we present this memorial as a symbol of high esteem in which we held your husband and your father.

After four uniformed soldiers drew back the heavy veiling from the monument, Mrs. Mamer rose to reply "Although deeply touched by this occasion, no greater pride will ever come in the lives of Patricia and me than that which we now enjoy. We are proud, because you – the friends of Nick – have paid to him a tribute that comes seldom in the lives of men."

Mrs. Mamer then presented the memorial to Major Sutherlin for "safe-keeping," a volley was fired by the squad of infantrymen and taps sounded. The ceremonies over, Colonel Orndorff shouted a sharp command that set in motion the parade of the 161st Infantry Regiment, members of which had stood at rest during the dedication. Governor Martin and his official party then turned to review the parade, which officially ended the ceremonies.

Chapter IX

Other Pre-World War II Activities

The Bigelow Johnson operation with three Eaglerock planes in 1928. *(Courtesy MAC, Libby photo L87-1.37559-28)*

Having already looked at some of the highlights of "the beginnings," the early National Guard, Nick Mamer, and airline activities, the need remains to document some of the additional commercial or general aviation activities in Spokane before World War II.

Firms like Inland Eaglerock Sales Co., Bigelow Johnson Flying Service, Mamer-Shreck Aviation Co. (Mamer-Shreck Air Transport), Connick Air Service, Burns & Lamb Co., Wallace Air Service, Wallace Aerial Surveys, Wallace Aeromotive, Budd Aircraft, Lamb Flying Service and Calkins Aircraft, to name a few, were all making history in Spokane during this growing period and probably didn't even realize it.

THE INLAND EAGLEROCK SALES CO.

This firm was housed in the first of three hangars built in 1928, several hundred feet east of the National Guard facility. I remember it as a kid when I was making model airplanes. An employee for the Alexander Eaglerock Company was the best scale model airplane builder in town. His 24-inch super grade scale model of a Curtiss Hawk (olive drab fuselage and yellow wings) won the contest sponsored by the National Aeronautic Association. In addition, he made for sale a number of 24-inch scale models, of less detail, but very attractive, of the Eaglerock plane, just like the big ones the company sold. This model had a dark blue fuselage and silver wings and was sold for eight dollars. I wanted one in the worst way, but couldn't come up with that much money from my *Saturday Evening Post* route. One kid in the neighborhood did

Carl Schirmer by an aircraft, 1930. *(Courtesy MAC, Montana Aeronautics Commission photographer, Mamer-Shreck Collection L84-256.100)*

get one for Christmas and was the envy of you know who. The Eaglerock plane was an open biplane with double cockpits and either an OX-5 or a Hisso V-8 engine. It was highly touted as a rugged dependable machine and said to be practically spin-proof.

On a certain occasion, Carl Schirmer took the beast up to test this characteristic. In the process, he got it into a flat spin that over-rode his ability to get it out, and he and the plane came down in a rotating, flat, tight spiral that ended in the telephone wires on the ground just south of the field. Carl lost an eye in the fiasco. Such an injury usually ended the career of a pilot (with the exception of Wiley Post), because the depth perception test was considered very important in the airman's physical exam. Not so with Carl Schirmer. His excellence as a pilot in the Guard Squadron, acknowledged skill as a commercial pilot and his leadership around the airport caused the Civil Aeronautics Administration to allow him to continue flying both at the field and later with Johnson Flying Service in Missoula. (During World War II he ran the Wallace Air Service operation while General Hillford Wallace was on active duty.) Other than the precious eye, Carl was not seriously hurt, but that, for all practical purposes, ended the expansion of the Eaglerock sales in Spokane.

John Dean, an old-time pilot who followed the Inland Eaglerock Sales Co. in the hangar and operated an airplane repair facility in 1929, recalled: "You could glide an Eaglerock until you got hungry." This may have been true, but the very name seems to be in conflict to me, not being sure whether it flew like an eagle or fell like a rock. Finally, this is the same hangar Roy Shreck had for years. It was condemned and torn down in 1972.

BIGELOW JOHNSON AVIATION COMPANY

The Bigelow Johnson Aviation Company, a provider of flight instruction and charter services, was formed in 1928 by H. W. Johnson and Edgar Bigelow, who was one of Spokane's well-known flyers. Bigelow was killed in 1931 while flying the airmail. His wife continued to operate the company until November 1935, when she sold her interest in the concern to Clare A. Hartnett and Herbert L. Budd. Both had been working for the company for several years. Budd, an experienced mechanic, became president. Hartnett had learned to fly under Bigelow and was also a lieutenant in the Washington Air National Guard. The firm occupied the middle "round roof" hangar just east of Inland Eaglerock (later Mamer-Shreck) and west of the Mamer (Paulsen) hangar. The same building was next occupied by Wallace Air Service (in 1936-39) before they built the larger quarters of Wallace Aeromotive east of the Northwest Airlines hangar.

THE BROWN BROTHERS' METALARKS

In 1930 and 1931, Thoburn and Bill Brown built three experimental metal aircraft in their father's "tin" shop in Spokane. The Brown family lived next to Vic Dessert at Liberty Lake during the summers, and the two senior boys were a little older than I. Naturally I followed their various innovative projects with great interest. These not only included the airplanes but also a "radical" frameless, light-weight aluminum bus, with a Ford V-8 engine, employing the then-new principle of a "monocoupe construction" where the skin imparts the basic strength to the structure. As I recall, the bus was made in the 300 block of East Sprague, while the planes were built in the shop at South 170 Post Street, next to the alley.

The Browns' first plane was a neat, compact, high-wing monoplane with a five-cylinder Le Blonde radial engine. It had a narrow, rather squared fuselage that could hold two or three people in tandem. The alumi-

The young Brown brothers stand beside their latest creation, *Metalark II*.

num skin was mostly corrugated for rigidity as was the custom in those days. Nick Mamer made the initial test flight in the *Metalark I* in March 1930. It was quickly sold and several years later was destroyed in a hangar fire.

As soon as the boys finished their first plane, they started working on their second machine. *Metalark II* was much more modern and more "sexy" in design than #I! It was a sleek, rounded-line, low-wing "racer" with a minimum frontal profile in-line engine (a four-cylinder Cirrus), and with wheel fairings to reduce the drag. Very similar designs later appeared in the limited displacement airplane racers, for example, Benny Howard's *Pete*, etc. *Metalark III* apparently followed, although I only remember *II* in construction. Both were sold to California pilots.

The Brown Brothers had hoped to form the Brown Metalplane Company to turn out these fine craft, but the Great Depression and the freshly discovered need for large amounts of capital turned them away from airplanes into the less costly field of light-weight truck bodies and aluminum trailers. Thus, from a rather humble beginning, the two Spokane brothers, with an intense interest and a faith in the new light metals, developed, over the years, a very successful aluminum fabrication business, climaxing in the massive Brown Industries, Inc., once one of the nation's largest truck-trailer body manufacturers. The principles pioneered and learned in the early airplane construction, and particularly triggered by the flight of Charles

Metalark I, above, was rather conservative compared to *Metalark II*, below.

A. Lindbergh, resulted in a dream-come-true for two fine Spokane "boys" and a valuable basic payroll for Spokane for a number of years.

Incidentally, Thoburn Brown confirmed to me he remembered Tom Symons's airplane on floats at Liberty Lake during the summer of 1920 or 1921. He, like many others, took a flight with Tom, who lived two houses away and undoubtedly received some inspiration from this towards the Metalark projects.

THE MAMER-SHRECK STORY

By 1934 the Mamer Air Transport Co. realized the battle was lost to Northwest Airways and sold their two Ford Tri-motors. Nick took a job as chief pilot on the northern route for Northwest, and Cip Paulsen decided to concentrate on his mining interest at Nugget Creek near Fairbanks. Cip purchased a very desirable Balanca Airmaster on floats with a 450-HP Wasp and gave up piloting himself in the interest of self preservation and hired a professional pilot named Gene Myring. Nick Mamer moved to Seattle, which was his Northwest Airlines home base, but spent every other night in Spokane. He was still keeping the basic Mamer Flying School activities going with a staff of faithfuls.

In 1929 the area was shaped as above. The first small Mamer hangar (black) is beyond the small houses next to the second Mamer Hangar (long white one), while the Spokane Airways hangar is just east, parallel to the tracks.

A good view of the hangar complex as it appeared in October 1931. By this time the Spokane Airways hangar had been dismantled and the National Guard headquarters building has a new addition. The old 1919 original hangar had not yet burned. Of the three new hangars beyond the Guard, the first was for the Alexander Eaglerock dealer, the next was for Bigelow Johnson (later occupied by the Wallace Air Service), while the last one was built by Mamer (and Cip Paulsen) to service the big Ford Tri-Motors. Several years later it was purchased by Louis Wasmer and operated by Al Connick. Claude Calkins then purchased it before he built Calkins Air Terminal. Beyond this hangar is the foundation for the start of the Airlines Terminal Building. Note: the first addition to the brick administration building is on the west and became the center section of the final and latest addition on the west of the building.

Mamer-Shreck Air Transport Company repair shop at Felts Field, 1940. *(Courtesy MAC, Forde photographers, Mamer-Shreck Collection, Libby photo L84-256.29)*

Lounge used by the Mamer-Shreck Air Transport Company repair shop at Felts Field, 1940. *(Courtesy MAC, Forde photographers, Mamer-Shreck Collection, Libby photo L84-256.29)*

According to a taped interview at one of Bill Toth's Old Time Pilots meetings, several years before this, a dapper "dude" by the name of Roy Shreck rode into the Mamer Flying School hangar on a Harley Davidson motorcycle and said he wanted to learn how to fly. After a couple of lessons, he decided to purchase a used plane and become a pilot. A professional pilot, that is. Roy's enthusiasm and interest apparently impressed Nick and eventually a partnership was worked out, operating under the name of Mamer-Shreck Air Transport. The Mamer name gave the public confidence in the firm, while the young, active partner provided the thrust that pushed the operation forward on all fronts. Roy Shreck did become an excellent professional pilot and businessman, and the two were associated together until Nick's untimely death in the Lockheed Zephyr in 1938. After this, Roy purchased the Mamer interest from Mrs. Mamer but kept the name for obvious reasons.

During the last half of the thirties, Mamer-Shreck became one of the leading operators at Felts Field and in 1939, with the newly created Civilian Pilot Training Program, had a fleet of four Taylor Cubs, two Luscombe (65), one Stearman, one Fairchild 24, one Fleet Trainer, and a Stinson. By 1939, "the Mamer-Shreck combined operations had logged 21,225 plane hours, trained 1,535 students and carried over 20,000 passengers without a single injury to any student or passenger." A picture on file shows the "members of the Mamer-Shreck Air Transport organization as of March 1940," listing Lloyd Woodward, P. Peters, Russell Bird, Noel Lempty, Roy Shreck, Lew Becker, Joe Kelly and Red Martin.

Much of what went on at Felts Field was not of general knowledge to the public, but one thing that everyone was aware of was the nightly flight of the "weather pilot" who, under contract, took the weather instruments aloft to gather data for the national weather system. Roy Shreck, replacing Ira Bortles, had established an outstanding record over a period of three years as a weather pilot by starting each flight on time and only missing one flight, and this was a result of equipment failure. Roy had indeed grown in a few short years from a fun-loving motorcycle kid to a respected professional pilot.

He became extremely well known, however, as a result of a flight that started a few minutes after midnight on Sunday, February 12, 1939. He took off from Felts Field at 12:29 a.m. carrying instruments that recorded air pressure, temperature and humidity at various altitudes above Spokane. Eighteen minutes later, Shreck contacted the airways communications station at Felts, reporting from 8,000 ft. that he had struck light snow above Spokane. At 1:08 a.m. he reported that he was heading west, but was being blown east by strong winds at 13,000 ft. At that altitude, he reported that ice was forming on his aerial and affecting radio transmission. His wife, who usually listened to him on the short wave radio (3105KC), heard him say about 1:20 a.m. that he was coming down and flying blind because of heavy fog. That was the last that was heard from him!

When he failed to return after the 4:00 a.m. deadline for his fuel, he was presumed down and an extensive search and rescue mission was started. The news of the favorite Spokane weather pilot being down traveled far and wide. Helpful people all over northern Idaho, eastern Washington and western Montana called in with reports. Details from these reports could fill a book by themselves, but a quick look at some of the headlines seems to tell the story of anxiety and concern of local citizens. My own neighbor, a real estate salesman, who knew nothing about airplanes, seemed compelled to start a scrapbook of clippings about his new hero. These headlines proclaimed, "Mystery Veils Fate of Weather Plane Pilot Shreck," "Missing Aviator Sought by 15 Ships," "Wife Got Last Message at 1:20 a.m.," "Reported Ice on Plane," "Reports Cover Wide Region," "Might be Buried in Snow," "Learned from Nick Mamer," "National Guard Unit and Volunteers Search for Roy Shreck," "Went Down Doing His Duty," "Sleepless Radio Operator Aids Search," "Wife of Missing Pilot Sure He Will Be Found Safe," "Shreck May Have Plunged

CHAPTER 9 – OTHER PRE-WORLD WAR II ACTIVITIES

Into Lake," "Weather Hampers Search," "Hunt for Flyer Still in Vain," "National Guard Planes Helpless to Aid Search," "Extensive Oil Slick Near Bayview is Found," "This Man Saw Plane in Trouble," "Has Been Missing 36 Hours at 12:30 p.m. Today."

And so went the news, and everybody was concerned. One young girl at Marycliff High School, Kathleen Corrigan, wrote such a thought-provoking essay about "My Friend in the Blue" that it was printed as a feature story in the paper. She described how each evening after finishing her "Now I lay me down to sleep routine," she turned her thoughts to the missing pilot:

> I hear him. I hear the motor of his plane sputter as it starts out and then warming up as it leaves the ground in favor of the sky. I listen anxiously until it soon gains momentum and resembles the contented purr of a giant cat. Higher and higher this man flies, wider and wider he circles, until my human ears can no longer catch the music of his mighty motor. And then I can only picture on the walls of my darkened room, this man-made bird, with its stiff wings and metal body. But most of all I wonder about "him" up there in the blue, balanced as it were, between the heaven of God and the earth of man. What does he think about – ponder over up there alone and free . . .

And thus, a young girl most vividly detailed her concern and what was on the minds of almost everybody. Will he come back? – And then the electrifying news appeared in the newspaper:

> SHRECK IS ALIVE Roy Shreck is Alive – reunited with his family in Spokane! He saved himself, conquering a wilderness to do it. He walked twenty-five miles through a heavily timbered, mountainous, snow-covered north Idaho region, and, on the verge exhaustion, found a haven Tuesday night in a woodcutter's cabin three miles from Wolf Lodge Bay on the east arm of Coeur d'Alene Lake.
>
> The Weather Bureau flyer, who had been missing more than 80 hours, was weak today, and his feet were badly swollen, but otherwise appeared to be in good health. For three days and nights he suffered almost unbearable hardships – he had no food, shelter or fire – but he battled his way to civilization through snow that was at times deeper than he was tall. His refuge Tuesday night was a little cabin home of Mrs. and Mrs. Nordahl Amundson, who took him to Coeur d'Alene this morning. . . He said, "Something sure guided me out, I didn't get so much as a pin scratch."

Shreck told his story to the *Chronicle*. The first news of his safety was flashed by Shreck himself, as he telephoned his wife from the home of his brother Ray in Coeur d'Alene that he was all right. He told how his plane "crashed into the side of a high mountain ridge, about twenty-five miles northeast of Wolf Lodge Bay. Ice forming on his plane caused the ship to crash." He reported he had plenty of gasoline left. The crack-up occurred at 2:15 a.m. Sunday. Shreck credited the heavy timber, which kept the airplane searchers from seeing him Sunday, Monday and Tuesday, with saving his life when his ice-laden plane went down. The trees broke the fall so when it hit the deep snow on the side of the mountain he was not injured.

Thus the story has a happy ending and Roy Shreck became a local hero in addition to, but not replacing, Jack Fancher and Nick Mamer. Later, after World War II, Roy sold the Mamer-Schreck business to Russ Swanson and, for a number of years, continued his charter activity out of Palm Springs, California. He finally met his end in his "Bonanza" on a ridge in Montana in 1976.

"Shreck is alive!" February 1939.

Roy Shreck in his more "mature" years (after World War II).

LYRICS from LONG AGO
by THELMA BLOOM
Quoted from the *Tri-county Tribune*, Monday, August 16, 1976 – page 7

This is an original poem written in the winter of 1938 - 1939 by Mike McCann, one of the oldtimers in the Deer Park area. The poem is nearly 100% true, even though it spells his name wrong.

This Har Schreck Fello

The luckiest guy In the world, by heck, Is this here fello they call Roy Schreck. He went up so high, he was yust a mere speck. And came down in a pile without breaking his neck. Now if that isn't lucky, I don't went a cent. Oh, I tell you this Schreck fello sure is some yont. It was his regular yob, this flying up high, To get dope on the weather up there In this sky. For nearly three years he'd been doin' this stuff. Some times it was easy, some times it was tough. He would go up et night with the sky black as yet.I tell you this Schreck is ell right, you bet.

Well, Saturday night he was feelin' yust fine, and he climed in his plane et twelve-twenty-nine. And that was the lest of him that was seen, And the last that was heard was et one nineteen. They tried end tried, but could not get e word. Oh, I tell you fellows, this Schreck is some bird. Well, by Sunday morning they knew he was lost, And must be found et any cost; So ten or a dozen planes took to the sky. They searched every mountain, down low end up high. But not a sign could they find that day. Oh, I think this Schreck fallo is sure gone to stay.

So Monday the search went on as before, But the sky got so cloudy, the vision was poor. So they gave up the search from the sir that day. And several ground parties got under way. On snowshoes end skis end rigs of ell kinds. Oh, l tell you this Schreck is e herd guy to find. Well, all of the people around here end elsewhere. Were sorry end sad end bewailing for fare, While his wife, Matte, at the Frankline Hell. Would yump up end down, some time she would bawl. But she never gave up in her faith he'd survive, She knew somehow bet nun, Schreck, was alive.

Well, Tuesday the hunt was a loss all around, Not a thing could be seen from the sky or the ground. But Wednesday 'bout noon all the struggle and strain. Was eased by a phone call from Coeur d'Alene, "What's that? Who is it? Am 1 hearing right?" Oh, this is the Schreck fello all right. Well, news of his safety spread wide and fast. And hundreds, yes thousands, of questions were asked. How did It happen and where did he land? A story would start and begin to expand, So no one could tell the wrong from the right, 'Till this Schreck fallo told of his plight. He said he'd ran into a real hurricane. And the wings got all iced from the snow and the rain. He'd have to turn back for he knew he was beat, So he stopped his ascent at thirteen thousand feet. He came down alright, but crashed in the woods. This here Schreck guy sure has the goods.

Well, he felt himself over, not a bruise or a scratch, Not one bite of food, not even a match. So he says to himself, "Well, here I am. I must figure some way to get out of this yam." Five feet of snow stared him right in the face, I tell you this Schreck was in a tight place. He knew he was east of Spokane, it would seem. Because he'd been on that radio beam. He walked all day Sunday, but 'twas all in vain, For Monday he had to return to the plane. But he got out his compass and started northwest I think this Schreck fello thought that was best.

Well, Tuesday the goin' sure was a fright. But he plodded along all that day and that night. He made a nest 'neath a side-spreading tree, But he dared not sleep, he might freeze, you see. And when dawn finally came, what a sight to behold. I bet you this Schreck fallo sure was some cold. So he started again with his hopes all renewed. And many and many a mirage he viewed, And at last the real thing came In sight. A cabin and people! Everything was all right. Well, those folks took him in and cared for his needs. Oh, I'm sure Schreck was thankful for these kindly deeds.

He stayed there that night and when the day came. They gave him a lift in to Coeur d'Alene. The details from there I'm sure you all know, But one thing more I must add also: I think matches and flares and a little food, to Will be part of Schreck's layout from now on.

THE DEMISE OF ROY SHRECK

Child Survives Crash Kills Roy Shreck

8/3/76

SILESIA, Mont. (A) — Searchers found a 9-year-old girl alive Monday afternoon beside the bodies of her parents and a 75-year-old pilot in the wreckage of an airplane that crashed near Silesia on Sunday.

Rescuers estimated the girl, Angie Loos of Cody, Wyo., had been pinned in the wreckage 26 hours.

A member of the rescue team said the youngster was fully conscious and coherent when found, but did not seem to realize what had happened to her parents.

She was listed in stable condition late Monday at a Billings hospital.

A reporter from a Billings television station, who ferried a paramedical team into the rugged crash site, said all four travelers were found in the fuselage of the single-engine Beech Bonanza.

The airplane, piloted by Roy Shreck of Cody, disappeared on a flight from Billings to Cody. Aboard were Donald Loos, 46, his wife Dorothy, 37, and Angie.

Observers at the site seven miles west of Silesia said the airplane apparently struck a tree, hit the ground, skidded about 100 yards through a hayfield and went over a cliff, landing on its nose.

The right wing apparently broke off on impact with the tree, followed by the tail section.

A rescuer said the child had been riding in a back seat and had been pinned in the wreckage. Debris from the airplane's interior blocked off her view of the bodies of the parents and Shreck.

The bodies of Shreck and the Cody couple were taken to a funeral home at Laurel, about 15 miles from the crash site.

A drenching rain covered the area the entire time the child was trapped in the fuselage, ranchers in the area said.

The airplane apparently was flying in low clouds Sunday at the estimated 3:45 p.m. time of impact.

* * *

This *Spokesman-Review* article dated August 3, 1976, described the accidental death of Roy Shreck and two passengers near Silesia, Montana. According to investigators, Shreck appeared to have been flying during cloudy conditions, struck a tree, hit the ground and skidded over a cliff.

SHOWING OFF FOR THE LADIES
HOLTER'S LAKE COEUR D'ALENE EMBARRASSMENT

Sunday morning, July 19, 1933, Sergeant Harold Hanson talked to Lieutenant "Charlie" Holter and convinced him they should make a slight detour in the scheduled mission flight path, so he could drop a note to several of his friends (girls) who were staying with Dr. Butt's daughter Harriett at Twin Beaches on Coeur d'Alene Lake. It was the custom for the 116th to have an early muster and drill each Sunday and then go through a practice flight exercise designed to perfect the skill necessary to be operationally effective.

This particular Sunday, the girls (Harriet Butts, Patsy Wilson, Madge Downey, Sarah Ferris and Frances Paulsen) were thrilled to see the low flying Douglass 0-38 pass overhead and wave to them. On the next pass the boys really gave them something to "oooh" and "aaah" about, and as they went from west to east, skimming the water, they made a steep bank at the point where Mrs. Paulsen's summer house is located, thinking this was where the lake shore turns north toward the city of Coeur d'Alene.

To his complete surprise (and embarrassment), the pilot suddenly realized there was still another point to round and that he was already in a very tight turn just above the water. Unable to change his course quickly enough, he was obliged to pull up as a 300-foot hill was in front of him. The plane apparently stalled and spun in coming to rest a few feet from shore in a twisted upside down mess of wreckage.

How the two survived is hard to understand. They had to be cut out of the ship. Their injuries were serious and both carried pins and plates for the rest of their lives. Since the impact had not killed them, they were lucky not to have drowned. Peacetime military flying had its hazards in those days. I mention this particular occurrence because in 1950 we built our Coeur d'Alene Lake home at this exact spot. I could look out the bedroom window and see the tree and the big rock where they hit not 50 feet away.

These photos and those on that preceding page are of Charlie Holter's and Harold Hanson's wreck at Twin Beaches on Coeur d'Alene Lake in 1933.

THE WALLACE FLYING SERVICE

The Wallace Flying Service was started by H. R. "Wally" Wallace in the mid-thirties, as was the Wallace Aerial Surveys. Wally had taken a reduction in rank with the 116th in late 1927, so he could enter Air Corps school at Sacramento in the special field of aircraft in support of the Army. He then went to the Presidio (Crissy Field) in San Francisco, which was the headquarters for the 15th Photo Squadron. After three years of active duty and two years with Pan Am, he returned to Spokane and the 116th in 1933. The commanding officer, Major Haynes, (Regular Army), was to be transferred to another station and Captain Lawrence Sherman would have normally been the remaining senior officer. As Lawrence was heavily involved in his civilian job and, since Wally had finished an extensive program of active military duty, it was agreed that "Sherm" would resign from the squadron, allowing Wally to be promoted to major and commanding officer, first of the photo section and then of the entire 116th.

Wally was so enthusiastic about aviation that after getting things settled in the Guard unit, he naturally wanted to work in his civilian job in the aeronautical field rather than his current assignment with Lacy Murrow in the Highway Department. As a result of this and his flying experience, he started the Wallace Air Service in the "round top" former Bigelow Johnson hangar, which was rented from the city. They did flight training and charter and service work much like Mamer-Shreck. Soon the government put out

Wallace Aero Institute & Wallace Air Service headquarters and flight school building at Felts Field, during World War II, July 22, 1941. *(Courtesy MAC, Libby photo L87-1.21194-41)*

Wallace Air Services flight line in 1937.

Wallace Aerial Survey's Fairchild and Travel-Air photographic fleet.

an invitation to bid on an aerial survey to map, catalog and monitor the tillable farm land in the United States. This was right down Wally's alley and he fortunately became the successful bidder. Wallace Aerial Surveys was formed and they purchased seven Fairchild model 70 planes with 450 P & W Wasps and built the hangar just east of the new Northwest Airlines unit to serve the fleet. More than 170,000 square miles were photographed and mapped during the period preceding World War II. (The scale was 1,000 ft. per inch. The map work from photos was done downtown in the old Holley Mason Hardware Building just south of the Northern Pacific Railroad on Howard Street.)

Since a very extensive shop had been set up to take care of the fleet of aircraft, it was soon discovered that planes from all over the Inland Empire and Alaska came for major repairs and service on Pratt & Whitney Wasps and Hamilton steel propellers. Harold Hahn was one of the highly regarded mechanics. Carl Schirmer ran the flight school and charter at Wallace Flying Service. With the coming of the Civilian Pilot Training Program before World War II, Wallace also set up a training school for the University of Idaho and Washington State College at the Pullman-Moscow Airport. (The service shop, the best in the area, later operated as Wallace Aeromotive, Inc. for a number of years after World War II.)

Looking at the picture of Russ Owen in the preceding chapter, standing proudly beside his new DeSoto Roadster in 1929, at the peak of his career, reminds me of his colorful but disappointing life. He was born in Indiana and when eight years old went to the county fair and saw his first airplane demonstration. He said, "The pusher with its rudder in the front, nervously moved across the infield of the racetrack, made a shaky takeoff, just cleared the fence and struggled into the blue." The crowd cheered and said, "What will they think of next?" Russ knew he was hooked – he was going to be a flier when he grew up!

Russ was in high school when World War I started. He attempted to make it into the Signal Corps Aviation Section, but ended up in another newfangled weapons section, the tanks. He was still stateside when the Armistice was signed, as was another frustrated soldier in his outfit, Dwight Eisenhower.

After the war Russ joined a flying circus as a mechanic and received a few lessons for his service. One night one of the flyers "belted one too many and made the bucket [jailed]. There was a very large crowd the next day and Russ was handed his helmet and goggles. That's how flyers were made in that long ago," according to the *Seattle Post Intelligencer*.

In 1925 Russ Owen was an instructor for Robertson Aircraft of St. Louis, along with another guy named Charles A. Lindbergh. By 1929 he was flying mail from Pasco to Spokane for Varney and then for United on the same run. By 1933 he had logged more than 5,000 hours without scratching any paint and was reported to have held a "master pilot's license," the highest rating attainable in American aviation.

In June 1930, with the fast living, his bubble finally burst and he lost his job and went to work at odd jobs for Mamer. Late in 1933, on a flight the short distance from Kellogg to Wallace, Idaho, during a severe ice storm, he spun in at Osborn and ended up in the hospital. The Department of Commerce didn't like the circumstances and revoked his flying license. In the hearing that followed, Russ claimed that he was being deprived of his livelihood by the action. In 1935 he was in the news again as the pilot for a new plane built in Marshal, Missouri, powered by a six-cylinder Plymouth automobile engine, which was to fly nonstop from Alaska to Spokane via the inland route.

The little high-wing ship with no struts held only 80 gallons of automobile gasoline and consumed four gallons per hour, thus giving it a 20-hour supply. Russ expected to make the trip in 18 hours. The calculated initial airspeed at 250 pounds over gross was 80 mph, which gradually would build up to 120 mph as the load burned off.

Well, the best-made plans often go astray! The destination was changed from Spokane to Seattle and the route was down the coast. Difficulties beset Owen from the beginning. His first attempt to take off at Anchorage on July 4th was unsuccessful. He discharged 10 gallons of gas and tried again with no luck. The Department of Commerce refused him an experimental permit for the flight, and he finally removed more fuel and "slowly rose into the air" on his third try. He circled the field for one hour and headed south, but was forced back by fog banks over Prince William Sound. After a try at flying a few letters down the Alaskan Coast and being blown from Ketchikan to Juneau, the backers called the whole thing off and the little Plymacoupe was retired to less demanding climes.

In 1937 Russ Owen went to China to help fight the Japanese, then held an assignment in the Navy during World War 11. He finally died on Skid Row in Seattle in 1962 with no money in his pockets, no papers, no keys and no known relatives. I wonder how many other aviation pioneers went through similar patterns in life.

BOY AND GIRL OVERBOARD

Another incident with tragic results happened in March 1935. Pilot Joe Miller rented a new Standard 200-HP plane from Bigelow Johnson to take some of his friends from the Medical Lake area for a ride. One of the four passengers seated in the small open-front cockpit had asked for "some experience in stunts" before the takeoff, but Miller said he was not stunting. All of a sudden, the seat belt holding two of the passengers broke in half and a 22-year-old young lady and a 23-year-old young man flew out of the plane while it was upside down. The results were earth-shaking! Pilot Miller said he "was attempting to make a mild wing-over when the gusty wind hit him and turned the plane almost upside down." He said the plane wouldn't spin over and started down, but when the bodies of the two were hurled from it, he was able to spin the plane back into position. Things like this never should happen, but they did during those early years of flying. I guess you would have to call it very painful growing pains!

It is impossible in a brief document such as this to cover all of the many events and incidents that occurred during these early years. Several thousand pilots were trained to fly at Felts Field. Many more thousands of Spokanites experienced their own aviation excitement and involvement, and hundreds of local pioneers engaged in aviation activities as professionals. I have only been able to touch on some of the highlights. Other little vignettes, both humorous and tragic, seem to come up occasionally and partially illustrate some of the happenings in those days.

In October 1934, four local men flew down to Portland for a Chevrolet automobile dealers' meeting. Their pilot was Ralph Shackleton of Newport, Washington, who had borrowed the Buhl aircraft from Nick Mamer for the flight because his own ship had been used for some Forest Service work by Mamer. It was being repaired and was late getting out of the shop. Mamer described him as "an aviator by experience." Others aboard were John A. Pring of Dishman near Spokane, Otis Parker of Sandpoint, Idaho, and Richard Thomas of Bonners Ferry, Idaho, all Chevrolet dealers.

Everything went well on the exciting journey until they started to land at Felts Field after dark and found "the dashboard lights had gone out." As a result, the pilot did what he felt was necessary and asked for one of his companions to light a match so he could see the instruments. The resulting flare of the match apparently blinded him and he "misjudged his landing speed and the plane flipped upside down," according to the local press. All but Parker were painfully injured but recovered. It was pointed out that the loaned airplane "had about a 40-mph higher speed than that of Shackleton's own ship. The Buhl was a total loss."

In the mid-thirties, the Felts Field Commercial Operators periodically held a Sunday air show. The purpose was to promote aviation in general and interest in learning to fly. A typical program of this type, described in the *Spokane Press* in 1937, invited the public to the local show. The build-up told how the six Spokane aviators scheduled to participate had a total of "over 18,000 hours, or 750 days" in the air. Below the pictures of the handsome young guys (bedecked in the usual leather jackets, "Scully" leather helmets, goggles and silk scarfs), the copy indicated the caliber of airmen who were to participate:

> Al Connick of the Connick Air Service, has had ten years of flying experience for a total of 2200 hours. He holds a transport flying license and learned his flying from Nick Mamer, Spokane's million-mile flyer. Connick will participate in the bombing contest and in the three-lap closed course race and will execute several dangerous maneuvers.
>
> Roland Lamb and Homer Burns of the B and L Flying Service each hold a Transport license. Burns will go through the maneuvers required of a pilot wishing a private license. Both will participate in the bombing and race.
>
> Lloyd Hardesty, holding a commercial license with approximately 350 hours, will fly a Stearman plane in the streamer-cutting exhibition and race. The plane will be donated by Roy Shreck, veteran pilot.
>
> Arnold Landry, Spokane garage-man and sportsman pilot, will participate in the race and bombing contest. The day's events will be judged by Tom Farbro, Airport Manager, and Al Coppula. Nick Mamer, pilot for Northwest Airlines with 10,000 flying hours, will announce events over the public address system. The show will start at 12:30 p.m. There will be no admission or parking charge!

THE LAMB FLYING SERVICE

Roland "Rollie" Lamb and Homer Burns formed the Burns and Lamb Flying Service in 1936 to commercialize on their newly-acquired pilot's licenses, and because they loved to fly. (Don't we all?) They had been associated before in the Burns Bus Line that ran from Spokane to Lewiston, Idaho, and other points. Both were involved in the activities around Felts Field. At first they operated out of the Bigelow Johnson hangar.

By 1939 Homer had joined the military and Rollie and his wife, Caryl, operated as the Lamb Flying Service, which offered flight training in a Taylorcraft and a couple of Porterfields. With the coming of the Civilian Pilot Training Program and the tremendous expansion in the number of pilots being trained due to the need for national preparedness, the Lamb operation and all the others in the business expanded rapidly. Rollie Lamb was a popular instructor at Felts Field during the late thirties because he had an easy going, unexcitable and pleasant personality that inspired confidence in his students.

By 1939 the Lambs had outgrown their initial quarters and planned a fine new facility just east of the Guard's metal hangar and west of the Mamer-Shreck. This was completed in 1940 and gave them the most modern commercial base of operations on the field. (After World War II, it was sold to Tom Day and then to Tom Price Jr.)

The finest pilot training that one could secure was in the military. The Army Air Corps had built the Randolph Field "West Point of the Air" complex in Texas, the Navy had Pensicola in Florida, and the Marines had Quantico, Virginia, and an arrangement with the Navy. Naturally any serious would-be flyer who wanted to be a military or airline pilot would try to take advantage of this training, which was said to be valued at $50,000 in 1938. Only the best could qualify and even they were thinned out with gusto. The graduates were indeed an elite group.

THE CIVILIAN PILOT TRAINING PROGRAM

At a lesser level and in order to form a broad pool of basically trained pilots for possible advanced training and some noncombat assignments, the Civilian Pilot Training Program or CPTP was initiated. In the two years before Pearl Harbor an ever-increasing number of young college men and women who applied for and who could pass the requirements were given the chance to become flyers under this government-sponsored program. It provided a tremendous opportunity not only for the students but also for the certified flying schools involved.

Lamb Flying Service's training planes in 1939. The planes are a Bird, Taylorcraft and Porterfield.

CHAPTER 9 – OTHER PRE-WORLD WAR II ACTIVITIES

Before this time, I had realized that I was not going to be able to attain my lifelong ambition of being a pilot in the Army Air Corps because of a little problem of 20-60 vision. As a result, I had taken a number of courses at the University of Washington in aeronautical engineering and in meteorology to prepare myself for flight training and hopefully a life of knowledgeable and safe private flying.

While still a student at the University of Washington, I took my initial flight instruction at Boeing Field from Elliott Merrill (#2903), owner of the Washington Aircraft Co. (along with Gill Cook) and soloed in an Aeronca Chief 50-HP after the usual eight hours. A few hours later, with the coaching of Elmer Hansen (#C32072) and Lee Clark (#24965), I passed my Class I-S and then Class II-S solo licenses and went on to my private license with flight tests by Emil Williams of the Seattle C.A.A. office. I was awarded license (#94032).

THE LADIES TAKE TO THE SKIES

Meanwhile, back in Spokane, my more-or-less steady girl, Milaine Jones, the granddaughter of Arthur D. Jones, a pioneer Spokane realtor, was trying to keep up with me by taking instruction from Rollie Lamb. By this time Rollie had purchased a new Luscombe 8A from Claude Calkins and Milaine soloed 26 days after I did and didn't wreck the plane. In fact, Rollie said she flew damn well!

Several other female pilots were at Lamb's at this time including Betty Monaghan, Marcella Fried and Alyce Robertson. A little later came Charlotte Semple (Witherspoon), and others.

The friendly competition went on between Milaine and me as we both worked toward our private licenses. In a gesture of daring (and to impress the young pilots), Milaine arranged to make a parachute jump by having her younger sister Patsy (Bacon) write a note to Rollie Lamb giving "parental permission" for the deed. (About 30 years later, Rollie found the note in his desk and sent it to us for preservation.) Dwight Calkins refused to fly the plane, an open cockpit Lamb Bird because he was afraid she might hurt herself. Some other guy flew the ship, but Bob Hairiston, later of the Spokane GADO office, FAA and an old family friend, Jack Clifton, were standing by to catch her as she landed on a barbed wire fence near Liberty Lake. For several years afterwards she would wake up in the night trying desperately to find the rip-cord handle!

In a letter he wrote to me after receiving the 1982 edition of this book, Kenneth L. Brinnon identified himself as the "other guy," stating: "I remember the chute incident very vividly, and recall Milaine's bravery and unhesitating action, as she climbed out of the cockpit of the Bird. . . . She turned around like a pro, faced the tail, smiled at me, lifted her arm in a wave, and without hesitation, dived into her new world."

After the parachute jump, I talked her mother into letting her go back to Seattle to enroll in the Washington Aircraft Seaplane School on Lake Union, where I could keep an eye on her! Occasionally that spring when I was out in my boat on Lake Washington trying to study, she would buzz by, "land" alongside and I would take the plane for a short one. It wasn't long before she passed her private flight test on floats and was awarded #94567 and had the thrill of taking up her first official passenger, her dad.

In 1940 after graduation, and when track season was over, we were married and both flew the Flying Club's Luscombe 8A (65-HP) until Bob Vandervert cracked it up (without insurance) not once, but twice. Prices in 1940 were cheap by today's standards. A new "cub" sold for about $1,200, and a Luscombe for $1,850. Solo time from a fixed base operator was $6 to $8 per hour and dual about $10. The Club's Luscombe only cost us $2 per hour plus fuel after you shared in the purchase price. How times and prices have changed!

Although Spokane never produced an Amelia Earhart, the city had its share of talented and dedicated women pilots in addition to my wife Milaine. They encountered an extra hurdle in learning to fly, as they

A picture staged the day after her 1940 parachute jump shows the author's bride to be, Milaine Jones, boarding a Shreck Stearman, according to Kenneth Brinnon. She did not wear saddle shoes for the actual jump.

were not always welcome as students in the flight schools. However, many persevered and won the men over, proving themselves as serious pilots.

As early as 1923, an "aviatrix" made a banner headline on the front page of *Spokane Press*. On August 14th, the paper declared AVIATRIX TO RECOVER and went on to recount the crash at Parkwater of

Innocent-looking enough, the young high-spirited, courageously-crafty Milaine Jones (McGoldrick), just prior to the planning stages of her stealthy parachute jump. The rest of the story follows.

THE REST OF THE STORY

Jim McGoldrick, Author
the *Spokane Aviation Story*

Dear Jim:

I was very thrilled to receive your book from my nephew, Bruce Lochhead, who keeps his Cessna 172 at Felts Field. This book was a birthday present to me. These incidents and re-calls which you so aptly describe, make me feel as if I an reliving those wonderful years.

The main purpose of this letter is to inform you of something, which I am sure will be quite valuable to you and Milaine I believe that Milaine will recall that big day of her Chute Jump. I am specifically referring to page 220 of your book. Quote: "some other guy flew the ship," and mentioning that Dwight Catkins refused to fly her for fear of her being hurt. He did not fly the BIRD. The "other guy" was Kenny Brinnon, pilot and flight instructor for Lamb Flying Service. I am sure that Milaine will recall the name. Bob Hairiston will confirm this.

It is true that Rol and Caryl Lamb and I refused to fly her for the jump, without her father's permission. She disappeared for two hours, and came back with a note supposedly from her Dad, giving her permission for said jump.

Incidentally, until reading your book, I thought that the note was genuine, and we did not realize that it was of her sister's authorship. (Incidentally, Caryl Lamb's name is spelled with a "y".) My wife, Jimmie, and I named our daughter after her.

I was thrilled to see Russ Owen's picture. He was my instructor when I started my flying in 1934, and it was in the Waco OK-5 owned by Bob Mckee.

I remember the Chute incident very vividly, and recall Milaine's bravery and unhesitating action, as she climbed out of the front cockpit of the Bird. (NC 933V), 4-POLB, Kinner B-5. She turned around like a pro, faced the tail, smiled at me, lifted her arm in a wave, and without hesitation, dived into her new world. It is true that Milaine did land on a barbed wire fence as confirmed by Bob Hairiston.

When I became co-pilot for Northwest Airlines, I gave instrument instruction to students of both Mamer-Schreck and Lamb Flying Service. I flew for Northwest for 30 years, retiring in 1970. I started on the DC-3 and ended up with the 707-320.

The Bird from which Milaine made her jump was owned by Rol Lamb. Shreck did not have a Bird. Milaine's picture on page 219 was taken with Shreck's Stearman for publicity purposes. Incidentally, I was vice president of the Aero Club of Spokane, p. 239, and our newspaper was assembled and printed by the very capable aviation enthusiast, Bob Roberts, who was Shaw and Borden's top printer.

My wife, Jimmie, and I are looking forward to the completion of your next book, and we want to thank you for your thoroughness on your research for your book, "The Spokane Aviation Story".

Sincerely, "some other guy"
Kenny Brinnon

The pilot/parachute jumper, and future Mrs. McGoldrick, Milaine Jones, posing on an aircraft in 1940. This was a promotional photo when Milaine was voted as the local rodeo queen. The aircraft is a Lusumbe 8A.

Daisy Smith, landlady of the California Hotel. The article described her as "Spokane's only woman aviator," who had been flying for two years. Daisy Smith's Curtiss plane was a total wreck and her injuries required surgery. Nick Mamer examined the wreckage and interviewed witnesses to determine the cause of the crash. He said "It was a plain case of motor stalling. She had flattened out in her glide too soon and, to make the landing field, gave the motor 'the gun' and lifted the nose of the plane too suddenly. The result was that the engine stopped . . . the machine fell into a tail spin and came down."

Unfortunately, future newspaper references to Daisy Smith involved activities other than aviation. The March 5, 1926, *Spokane Press* bore a headline, "FEDERALS GRAB WOMAN AVIATOR ON RUM CHARGE." A prohibition raid on the California Hotel yielded "a quantity of alleged bonded liquor" and reported that Daisy Smith had spent 60 days in jail in 1924 on a similar charge.

The next Spokane woman aviator to gain significant local press attention was Maude B. McClaine, who in 1929 was the first woman in Washington (according to her newspaper obituary, March 12, 1980) to receive a private pilot's license. She was the wife of A. Fielding McClaine, a petroleum executive, and was active

Maude B. McClaine, wife of Fielding McClaine, earned her pilot's license in 1928. Her co-pilot and instructor was Nick Mamer. She was the first woman to obtain a limited commercial license in the Pacific Northwest. In 1930 there were only 24 such licenses in the United States. *(Courtesy MAC, Libby photo L94-9.82)*

in Spokane society. According to the newspaper account, she soloed after only 11 hours of instruction at the Nick Mamer Flying School to become Spokane's first graduated woman pilot. She received a limited commercial license in 1930, one of only 25 American women holding such a license at the time. I remember Maude McClaine as one of Spokane's first and most attractive female pilots and a friend of my parents in the late 20s and 30s. I can recall her flying an open biplane at the Mamer Flying Service at Parkwater.

Local women's interest in aviation may have received a boost in 1933 when Amelia Earhart made a much-publicized visit to Spokane, although she came as a passenger and not a pilot. On the evening of January 30, she arrived in a Ford Tri-motor piloted by H. B. Reuschenberg. The other passenger was Colonel L. H. Brittin, vice president of Northwest Airways. The three were scouting the proposed route for Northwest's airmail service from Minneapolis to Seattle. After spending the night at the Davenport, the party announced they were departing in the morning from Felts Field in spite of a blinding snowstorm. In reality the snow storm proved to be too great and they stayed over another night. A gushing interview in the *Spokane Press* paid more attention to her attire and femininity than to her aviation achievements.

Spokane women pilots continued to attract press attention, partly as novelties. One such lady was Alma Heflin, a winsome young teacher at Audubon School, whose flight achievements the newspapers followed with great interest. Beginning in 1934, she took flight lessons at Felts Field from Lt. Clare A. Hartnett (a man, despite his feminine-sounding first name). During the summer, Alma also worked as a bookkeeper for the Bigelow Johnson Company, a charter and flight instruction company at Felts Field. On June 20, 1934, she described in the newspaper a lesson during which she flew with Lt. Hartnett to Cheney to deliver a hat to her sister. As she got into the back cockpit of a Student Prince, Hartnett asked the petite Alma if she had enough cushions to see over the cockpit.

Miss Heflin's article also gave a detailed description of what may have been a fairly typical lesson. While searching for Four Lakes, she let her attention wander from elevation, and Hartnett yelled into the speaking tube: "You're diving! Get the nose up!" Hartnett decided to give Alma's sister and her friends a thrill as the plane approached the Cheney landing field by taking over the controls and rolling the plane. He kept the controls for the landing. Alma handed over the hat to her sister and tried to keep a lot of curious kids from getting too close to the propellers. As they took off for the return to Spokane, Lt. Hartnett told her to "wig-wag" the wings in farewell.

A November 19, 1934 newspaper clipping pictures Alma Heflin beside a plane and announces that she will be honored at a luncheon of the Club for receiving a permit to solo. On October 16, 1935, the paper announced that she had soloed and graduated from the flight training program at Bigelow Johnson. The article described her landings: "On descending from great heights she guided the plane to three happy landings, each successively better than its predecessor, for which she was given an ovation by airmen of the field." A month later, Clare Hartnett became part owner of Bigelow Johnson. Alma Heflin was active in the Spokane Flying Club, in which she appeared to be the only woman member in 1935. In 1936 she was instrumental in planning a women's air show in Spokane. Later she became director of sales promotion and publicity for the Piper Aircraft Company.

Women would have enjoyed participating in the various air shows and races held around the country, but were usually excluded by the men who made the arrangements and decisions. Therefore, the ladies held their own shows. As early as 1929, women aviators formed a national club, the Ninety-Nines, choosing the name because they had 99 charter members. Amelia Earhart was the first president. Spokane was one of the cities with a chapter. That same year, on November 2, a women's air race was held at Curtiss Field, Long Island. The journalist and humorist Will Rogers dubbed it the "Powder Puff Derby," and the name stuck for the subsequent women's air races, which were held for many years in various places.

Amelia Earhart. *(Courtesy Library of Congress)*

CHAPTER 9 – OTHER PRE-WORLD WAR II ACTIVITIES

On Sunday, June 28, 1936, the Associated Women Pilots of Spokane hosted what the newspapers called the "All Women's Air Frolic" at Felts Field. Women from all over the Northwest competed in a program of stunting, racing and exhibition flying. Among the Spokane participants were Alma Heflin, Jean Whitman, Shirley Fish, Edna Anderson, Dorothy Sartori, and Mary Towne. Mayor Arthur Burch and Vic Dessert were the first to purchase advance tickets, and the Aviation Committee of the Chamber of Commerce lent support to the event. However, the festivities were marred by two crashes of women en route to participate, one at Cheney and another near Camas. In both cases, the women were slightly injured but no one was killed. Additional problems occurred on the day of the Frolic, with several planes grounded by engine problems.

The event carried on, however, with the papers reporting about 1,000 spectators in attendance. Edna Barric Anderson of Missoula won the sweepstakes prize and Besse Halladay of Portland came in second. They received their trophies from Mayor Burch.

Although many of Spokane's women pilots were recreational flyers, quite a few were professional and even connected to the military. A June 16, 1998, *Spokesman-Review* feature article by columnist Doug Clark recounts the flying career of Millie Shinn, a "living legend" in Spokane women's aviation. She was a regional leader of the Ninety-Nines who racked up "hundreds of air hours in dangerous search-and-rescue missions" over the years.

Millie Shinn began taking flying lessons in Billings, Montana, in 1940. When the Civilian Pilot Training Program was formed early in World War II to increase the pool of pilots, only men were welcome to apply. Then in 1941, the program in the Northwest agreed to admit one woman for every 40 men. Although her instructor vowed to wash her out in six hours and tried to scare her off by performing loops and rolls in the open cockpit Rearwin Sportster, Millie proved her mettle and became a pilot. She was one of five Northwest women accepted into the WASPS (Women Air Force Service Pilots) and flew with the Montana Civil Air Patrol during the 1950s.

Even her marriage was related to aviation. Millie's husband, Shirl Shinn, also a pilot, enhanced the chances for his proposal by painting "Millie B." on his Fairchild PT-19.

Jean Smith Landa was another important Spokane woman pilot who began her flying career during the period covered by this book. A graduate of Central Valley High School, she attended Stanford University and graduated from the University of Washington. She took flight lessons at Felts Field and was the first female to take advanced aerobatics training in a program sponsored by Gonzaga University. Landa earned her commercial pilot's license in 1939 and was required to sign a pledge promising to serve in case of war. This led her to participate in the WASPS during World War II. She also taught Air Force cadets at Washington State College.

Another legendary Spokane aviatrix was Louise Prugh Hutchinson, whose career was described by Rob McDonald in the *Spokesman-Review*, July 9, 2003. She first started flight lessons early in World War II, but her actual flying career was interrupted by an assignment to train flight attendants in New York. She was soon married, started a family, and began a teaching career in home economics at Eastern Washington University. She resumed her flying and even took students on charter flights to study interior design or visit textile mills. Like Millie Shinn, Louise Prugh Hutchinson was a member of the Ninety-Nines.

Last but not least was Gladys Dawson Buroker, celebrated during the 1930s for her barnstorming, parachute-jumping and wing-walking. She went on to train pilots at Farragut Naval Base during World War II. In 2000 she was one of seven Americans to receive the Elder Statesman of Aviation Award from the National Aeronautic Association.

SPOKANE AVIATOR
Published by AERO CLUB of SPOKANE

Vol. 2, No. 3   FELTS FIELD---SPOKANE, WASHINGTON   March, 1940

Roland Lamb to Build New Hangar

The Lamb Flying Service has obtained space for building a new hangar on Felts Field and announces the construction will start shortly after the first of March.

Roland's new location is just east of the National Guard buildings. The new 76x100-foot hangar will be modern in appearance (somewhat similar to the Northwest building) and will include a comfortable waiting room.

The Budd Aircraft has reserved space the new hangar and plans a complete plane repair service.

Major Wallace to Give Talk at Aero Club

Major Wallace, commander of the local squadron of the National Guard, will tell the membership of the problems and training of the flying members of the National Guard at the March 7 meeting.

Major Wallace has invited the Aero Club to inspect the National Guard buildings and equipment at any time convenient to us.

Boeing Plant May Leave Northwest

Boeing Aircraft recently announced plans are being formulated for moving its plant to some other location. San Francisco or Los Angeles were mentioned as possible locations.

By the way, why wasn't Spokane mentioned in the likely locations? Surely Spokane's plentiful supply of cheap power, its inland location (though only a short flight to the Coast), its comparative freeness from fog conditions should have been good talking points in our favor.

Ladies Earn Their Wings

The young ladies pictured here (from top to bottom, Betty Monaghan, Marcella Fried and Milaine Jones, and Alyce Robertson) are but a few of the girls who have earned their wings this year. And they have done a swell job of it too.

Betty Monaghan at 16, is the youngest girl to ever solo from Felts Field. Marcella Fried earned her solo license on February 26, of which she is rightfully proud. Milaine Jones not only solos but has a parachute jump to her credit. Alyce Robertson is now showing the boys at Billings, Montana, how flying should be done.

Another local lady, Mrs. G. W. Schaffer, not satisfied with the 14 consecutive loops she did recently, took off last week and made 40 loops in a row. Few men will challenge that record.

REGULAR MEETING
Thursday March 7, 8:30 P. M.

Two women aviators photographed at Felts Field. *(Courtesy MAC, Mamer-Shreck collection)*

In talking about women in aviation, we shouldn't overlook pioneer flight attendants. In those days, they were called airline hostesses and later, stewardesses, and were usually required to be registered nurses. Just as with women pilots, the newspapers made quite a fuss over them. An article on February 11, 1935, announces that "two Spokane graduate nurses, Miss Marguerite Cordier and Miss Gladice Putnam, will enter the service of the United Airlines on Friday, both having signed up as stewardesses on passenger runs in the northwest." Miss Cordier was a graduate of St. Luke's School of Nursing and Miss Putnam of Sacred Heart. Their uniforms were typically tailored suits, sensible shoes and small hats. The early United Airline stewardesses even wore neckties. The attire was definitely professional rather than glamorous.

Photos and articles about two other stewardesses, Marian Bennett and Ellen Hughes, appeared in the papers several times. They were described as Spokane's first stewardesses with United's Pasco and Seattle route. Miss Bennett was later singled out as a heroine in a non-fatal crash of a Boeing monoplane near Selleck, Washington.

THE CALKINS STORY

To illustrate how fast things can happen in aviation, I am reminded of Claude Calkins. One sunny afternoon he was driving out east Trent Avenue when he noticed a sign that read "Learn to Fly." He turned left on an impulse and ended up at Felts Field for the first time, where he talked to Roy Shreck. Roy said, "Would you like to take a lesson?" Claude said, "Yes, why not!" – and things started to happen. Claude, who was more than a grown boy at the time, liked his first lesson so much he went home and told his two six-foot sons, Dwight and Ozzie, about it and suggested they also learn to fly.

After purchasing his first aviation magazine, he noticed an advertisement for the new Luscombe All-Metal Two-Placer. The ad invited "Dealer Inquiries," so the long-time farm-machinery manufacturer called the factory and ended up with the franchise and the first aircraft on the way. He got so enthused he bought Al Connick's hangar from Louis Wasmer. In a short time almost all the flying schools had a Luscombe or two.

The Civilian Pilot Training Program expansion interested Claude enough to decide to build his own airport on land he owned north of the city at the present site of Northtown Shopping Mall. After all, it was quite simple, he just had driver Henry Johnson knock out about 5,000 feet into the wind in the big Le Tourneau and, there she was, the largest privately owned airport in the area! The new field was called Calkins Air Terminal and it was a great help in the pilot training program that preceded World War II. The heavy traffic at Felts Field required the use of many other practice fields like Mead (improved by Wallace Flying Service), Deer Park, Weeks Field in Coeur d'Alene, and others in the Spokane Valley.

My own first experience at Calkins Air Terminal was in May 1941, several weeks before it was officially opened with a gala celebration. My bride and I rented the Fairchild 24 from Shreck and flew over to take a look. We were impressed with the size and overall appearance from the air. After landing, the "veteran pilot" let it get away from him and a mild but uncontrolled ground-loop resulted in the roll out. My three passengers were unaware that I wasn't really just turning around on the smooth sand runway, so I wasn't too embarrassed.

After take-off from Calkins we flew out over the new "Sunset (Super) Airport" and could plainly see the outline of each of the three runways then under construction. That May of 1941, little did any one of us know what was going to happen on that fateful Sunday, December 7th.

WALLY HAGIN, FIRST AFRICAN AMERICAN IN THE STATE OF WASHINGTON TO EARN HIS PILOT'S LICENSE

Wally Hagin, one of Spokane's more ambitious and diversified men, left his mark on the city in many ways, but, most importantly for the purposes of this book, he was the first African American in Spokane's history to earn a pilot's license. Wally was born in Butte, Montana, in 1915. Three years later, his family moved to Spokane. Other than leaving for occasional work or educational purposes, Hagin spent most of his life in Spokane.

Following his graduation from North Central High School, Wally enrolled in the University of Minnesota, where he studied to become a mortician. When no Spokane funeral homes would hire him, he found work in Seattle, later joining the Al Freeman Big Band as a trumpeter. After a year with the band, Hagin became one of the few African American students at Gonzaga University. Sometime during the late 1930s, Hagin's physics professor encouraged him to take up flying, which he did, subsequently earning his commercial pilot's license. Hagin spent World War II in Spokane flying for the Civil Air Patrol.

Following the war, Hagin operated a photography business and also worked at the Bon Marche and J. C. Penney stores. Besides music and flying, one of his passions was photography. By the time of his death in 2006, Hagin had taken over 13,000 Spokane-area photos depicting a wide range of the city's African American history. Prior to his death, his entire photo collection was acquired by the Northwest Museum of Arts and Culture (MAC).

"THE SUPER AIRPORT"

Toward the end of the 1930s, with Felts Field busy with general aviation, military and airline traffic, and with the facilities in reasonably good shape, the Spokane Chamber of Commerce members again started

Wally Hagin in a biplane taken during his second year of training in the Civilian Pilot Training Program at Felts Field. *(Courtesy MAC, Hagin Collection, L97-56.4)*

The 32nd Aviation Squadron at Geiger Field in 1942. *(Courtesy MAC, Libby photo, L96-1.10)*

to look into the future of aviation. The very active manager, Jim Ford, described the situation this way:

> To realize the importance of this [the proposed new "Super Airport"] consider that up to the time of development of aviation there were three modes of transportation – railroads, highways and water. Spokane was an important railroad center and had developed into a great highway center, but Spokane would never have water transportation. Transportation brings business, commerce and industry. It builds cities. We were what you might call a two-thirds city from a transportation standpoint. In other words, we had two out of three important modes of transportation. Now a new and revolutionary mode of transportation was coming in by air. Spokane must become an important air transportation center. It was a question of whether Spokane would slowly slip and have only two out of four major forms of transportation. To that end, we must have a new modern airport that would handle the latest and best equipment available.

The Chamber of Commerce induced the Civil Aeronautics Administration and the two airlines serving Spokane to make a survey to determine the best location for a new "super airport." Their report stated that the logical location was in the vicinity of Cheney Junction. No exact location was specified. The county commissioners were induced to purchase the land since all of it was in the county. In 1938 the location of the new Sunset Airport, as it was first called, was established. By early 1940, a Works Progress Administration project was started to clear and level the land for the runways. Soon, with war clouds forming, the Army Air Forces took over the job and changed the name to Geiger Field.

We have seen how the Spokane Chamber of Commerce was active in successfully promoting aviation in the area from the start. Some of the chairmen of the Aviation Committee of the Chamber that I recall in this period before World War II were Vic Dessert, Joe Albi, Phil Garnett, Hillford Wallace, Eustus Le Master and Harold "Air Express" Jones.

Memorabilia and Miscellaneous

Note from the publisher: Because Jim McGoldrick has been involved in so many interesting aviation-related endeavors, received numerous awards, acquired many friends and led such an interesting life, we prevailed upon him to compile a sampling in this final chapter.

Jim and Milaine McGoldrick (pilot and co-pilot) dressed for a party, pose with the family seaplane, a N-7911-V, at their Lake Pend Oreille home base. They are about to depart for Flathead Lake, Montana, to attend a wedding reception. They, like many Alaskans, used their Cessna 180 instead of a car or boat to visit friends, run errands, commute to work or just have fun.

THE FUDPUCKER WORLD AIRLINES SUCCESS STORY

Once upon a time (sometime in 1969), there was a group of business executives who traveled the nation on behalf of their companies. They traveled on airplanes hither, thither and yon, promoting their various businesses. The more they traveled, the more they were faced with flight cancellations, overbooked aircraft, substandard service and cold food, which seemed to be the norm at that time. In their unrelenting desire to upgrade the standards of the entire airline industry and improve the lot of their fellow travelers, the idea of the mythical Fudpucker World Airlines (FWA) was born in a bar one night with a bent of humor and absurdity.

The company colors became battleship gray and black. The founders established the first board of directors and business cards were printed, as well as passes to the famous Fudpucker World Airlines' cockpit club with locations in every major city throughout the world.

The airlines' official motto became "Serving the world with the famous Fudpucker Flying Machine," which, incidentally, was a hand-shovelled, coal-fed, steam-powered unit. To quote from the cover of a Fudpucker family cassette tape, "The Fudpucker Flying Machine has been Certified to be 100% smog free, no diesel exhaust or dumped fuel mars its flight. Only a gentle mist of pure water marks its path. Parched areas the world over are bidding for opportunities to be in the flight path of this remarkable flying machine. Environmental engineers acclaim it as the easiest plane to clean. The bare metal on its seats has proven less of a dust catcher."

According to the CEO of Fudpucker World Airlines, it was, at one time, recognized throughout the entire world. During the years of Jim McGoldrick's presidency, it was declared the official airline of the electronic industry.

Jim McGoldrick was fortunate enough to have received one of the first membership cards to the much sought after Fudpucker World Airlines L.T.D. Cock Pit Club, which to this day he still treasures.

J. P. MCGOLDRICK REALIZES A LIFE AMBITION WITH THE FAMOUS FUDPUCKER WORLD AIRLINES

J. P. McGoldrick, the president and CEO of Fudpucker World Airlines, (FWA) standing by the door of his Beach Bonanza. FWA was founded in 1969 and based out of Felts Field in Spokane.

FUDPUCKER WORLD AIRLINES
AHEAD OF ITS TIME IN INNOVATIVE DESIGN

On December 6, 1971, following a meeting with J. P. McGoldrick, two aerospace test pilots from the Los Angles Division of North American Rockwell sent McGoldrick this displayed letter and photo of the above FWA SST proposed jet airliner. Based on the content of their letter, this appeared to be a deviously flattering attempt to receive honorary captain status with FWA, which they were immediately granted.

Los Angeles Division
North American Rockwell

International Airport
Los Angeles, California 90009
(213) 670-9151

December 6, 1971

Mr. J. P. McGoldrick, President
Fudpucker World Airlines
Terminal Box 3047
Spokane, Washington 99220

Dear Jim:

As two old, broken down test pilots who with any smarts at all could now be proudly wearing the four gold stripes of an FWA captain, N. D. and I were honored to meet you during our recent B-1 presentation at Fairchild Air Force Base. It is great transportation companies like yours that we in Aerospace look to for the leadership necessary to restore America's sharp, cutting edge of technology.

Weighted down as you must be with the burdens of future route expansion and equipment planning, we hope that the enclosed proud picture of an FWA SST will help qualify us as honorary captains of your great airline.

Very truly yours,

H. C. Cotton
B-1 Program Development

HCC:aj

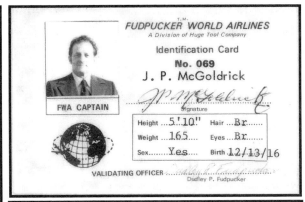

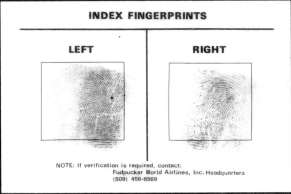

**Jim McGoldrick's original
FWA photo I.D. card, issued before he
attained the status of FWA's CEO.**

CHAPTER 10 – MEMORABILIA AND MISCELLANEOUS

THE FUDPUCKER WORLD AIRLINES HAD EVERYTHING

Following J. P. McGoldrick's retirement from FWA, he was replaced by John and Ann Schafhausen who immediately, following their takeover, initiated numerous changes and upgrades to FWA, including the following lines of fashionable apparel and accessories. Jim respectfully thanks and appreciates the new level of perfection brought to FWA by the Schafhausens. To those new to aviation, John Schafhausen is famous in aviation circles for his P-51 and his F4U-7 Corsair which he piloted in the filming of *Ba Ba Black Sheep*.

ORDERING INFORMATION

1. Please type or print clearly to avoid errors in delivery. If ordered by you and shipped to another person, please indicate both addresses.
2. Be sure to check over your order for correct identification, item number, quantity, cost, etc.
3. If additional space is required to accommodate your selection, please list on separate sheet of paper.
4. When sending in your order, enclose check, money order or traveler's check payable to R.P. Tool Company.
5. Average delivery time is about 4 weeks from the time the order is received.
6. FWA guarantees your complete satisfaction with every item or your money back. Each item is accurately described and illustrated — each item is fully warranted by the manufacturers and by FWA.
7. All orders require a $1.00 mailing and handling charge.
8. All orders should be sent direct to:
   Fudpucker World Airlines
   P.O. Box 3606
   Terminal Annex
   Spokane, Washington 99202

FUDPUCKER WORLD AIRLINES
TERMINAL BOX 3606   SPOKANE, WASHINGTON 99220

ORDER FORM
PRINT CLEARLY
NAME_____
STREET_____
CITY_____ STATE_____ ZIP_____

PLEASE RUSH ME...
quan.
- ☐ #1 Vinyl garmet bags $_____
- ☐ #2 Tote bags $_____
- ☐ #3 Sweatshirts   S,M,L,XL $_____
  (MINIMUM ORDER 1 GROSS) CIRCLE PROPER SIZE
- ☐ #4 Cotton T-shirts S,M,L,XL $_____
- ☐ #5 Slumber shirts   S,M,L,XL $_____
- ☐ #6 Lighters $_____
- ☐ #7 Bumper stickers $_____
- ☐ #8 Business cards $_____
- ☐ #9 FWA Stationery $_____
- ☐ #10 Windbreakers   S,M,L,XL $_____

ENCLOSED IS $_____
(include $1.00 for handling with ea. order)
make checks payable to R.P. TOOL CO.

send to   FUDPUCKER WORLD AIRLINES
no stamps   P O BOX #3606
  please   TERMINAL ANNEX
           SPOKANE, WASHINGTON 99202

IT'S A FUDPUCKER WORLD

FWA

FUDPUCKER WORLD AIRLINES

...classy brochures and numerous company promotional accessories...

JIM McGOLDRICK – SPOKANE AVIATION

...stewardesses...

...crew members...

...newsletters...

page 214

CHAPTER 10 – MEMORABILIA AND MISCELLANEOUS

GOOD THINGS COME TO OLD FUDPUCKER PILOTS AND THEIR ASSOCIATES – HONORS AND OTHER EVENTS

Monday, April 12, 1965 — The NORTHWEST FLYER — Page 3

Spokane's 1965 Pilot Of The Year

JIM P. McGOLDRICK is shown holding the Pilot of The Year trophy he recently received. 1964 was the first year for this trophy to be awarded and it went to Will Alton of Spokane, whose name is inscribed on the front of the trophy. In the very near future, Jim's name will be added—the permanent trophy has been on display at Felts Field. The Beechcraft in the background is Jim McGoldrick's and practically his only mode of travel away from Spokane.
—Photo courtesy N.W. Electronics Inc., Spokane

... awards ...

. . . more awards . . .

Flying Patrol Veteran Honored

Retired Brigadier General H. R. Wallace is shown receiving the trophies for the "Spokane Pilot Of The Year," from James P. McGoldrick. This award is given annually to a non-commercial pilot who has made a distinct contribution to Aviation and it was awarded to him recently at a Pilots meeting in Spokane. These trophies were originated by Carl Litzenberger of Endicott, Wash., also a veteran pilot, and have been given annually for 10 years. The small trophy remains in Gen. Wallace's permanent possession. The larger one is kept for one year and then passed on to the next winner.

"Wally", as he is affectionately known, was first involved in aviation in World War I. He was a mechanic at that time but learned to fly in 1920. He accumulated 11,500 hours of flying time since then. After World War I he joined the Washington Air National Guard and worked his way up from enlisted man to command of the unit. He served in World War II and was in charge of Photo Reconnaissance training in the Air Force. He had considerable civilian experience with this when he operated Wallace Aerial Surveys at Felts Field prior to World War II. He has been retired for 25 years and while he maintains a keen interest if flying, he is no longer actively engaged in it. This award is a fitting tribute to the man who is considered "Mr. Aviation" in Spokane.

McGoldrick, shown above presenting him with his trophies, is also an earlier winner of the trophy, a former president of the Chamber of Commerce, owner of Northwest Electronics, a member of many Aviation organizations and an avid flyer in his own right. Flying Patrol members who have won this award besides Wallace are Norman Majer, Charles Walters and Bill Toth.

. . . good press relations . . .

THE INTERNATIONAL NORTHWEST AVIATION COUNCIL
INAC'S ROLL OF HONOR

• INAC's Aviation Roll of Honor was established August 23, 1974, by the INAC Board of Directors. Each year one or more recipients of the honor are chosen by members of the board from nominees submitted by INAC members. Although not limited to the following criteria, selection is generally based on a person's promotion of the field of aviation in the INAC area of influence and promotion of public understanding and acceptance of aviation's value to the community. A book containing information about recipients of the Roll of Honor Award, and photographs of each, will be displayed in the Pacific Northwest Aviation Historical Foundation in Seattle, Washington, also at each INAC Convention.

... international attention and recognition ...

THE 1987 ROLL OF HONOR AWARD FOR DISTINGUISHED SERVICE TO AVIATION AWARDED TO DONALD W. NYROP

DONALD W. NYROP

Chairman of the Board & Chief Executive Officer, Northwest Orient Airlines

Born in Elgin, Nebraska, Nyrop received his undergraduate degree from Doane College at Crete, Nebraska. He earned his law degree from George Washington University. In 1942 he was appointed special assistant to the chairman of the Civil Aeronautics Board. From 1942 to 1946 he served with the U.S. Air Force attaining a rank of Lt. Colonel.

Nyrop was named deputy administrator of the Civil Aeronautics Administration in 1948. Later, by Presidential appointment, he served as Administator of the Civil Aeronautics Administration. In 1951 to 1952 Nyrop served as Chairman of the Civil Aeronautics Board.

Prior to joining NWA as president in 1954, Nyrop practiced law with a private firm in Wasington, D.C. After serving as Northwest's president for 22 years, Donald W. Nyrop was elected Chairman and Chief Executive Officer of Northwest Orient Airlines on October 1, 1976.

Nyrop retired from the airline January 1, 1979.

Donald Nyrop was a respected colleague of Jim.

THE 1987 ANNUAL ACHIEVEMENT AWARD
AWARDED TO JAMES P. MCGOLDRICK

Sponsored by
Lucile M. Wright in the name of General William Mitchell

JAMES P. McGOLDRICK II

Jim was born December 13, 1916 in Spokane, Washington and raised in Spokane.

His enthusiasm and love for aviation was manifested at an early age at Felts Field Airport where he spent most of his spare hours. This dedication and romance with aviation was to have a profound influence on the development and direction of aviation and airport developments in Spokane.

He acquired his pilots license #94032 in 1939 one year prior to his wife Milaine earning her license.

During WWII, Jim was a civilian radio engineer for the United States Air Force at Wright Field, Dayton, Ohio and later at the Spokane Air Depot which became Fairchild Air Force Base. He was instrumental in the research and development of the I.F.F. (Identification Friend or Foe) channels which led to the transponder as we now know it.

As a third generation Spokane businessman and owner of Northwest Electronics, Jim was in a position to substantially influence the aviation programs in Spokane. He accomplished this by generous use of his time and airplanes to support the travels of the officials and others in Spokane. These travels to other cities and events resulted in the proper and timely development of Spokane International Airport and the establishment of administrative authority.

He worked diligently as a member of the Spokane Chamber of Commerce Aviation Committee serving as its Chairman during the critical emerging years of the airport authority activity.

He was named Spokane Pilot of the Year in 1965.

Jim was President of the Spokane Chamber of Commece 1969-1971. He is a 13 year member of the Spokane Airport Board and has served as Chairman of the Board for 2 terms.

Jim was a lifelong friend of INAC's Roll of Honor recipient General Hilford R. Wallace and dedicated many years to making Wally's declining years comfortable and fulfilling.

In 1986 Jim was honored by the Spokane Airport Board and Staff by dedicating the new Spokane International Airport commercial center as the McGoldrick Aero Mall and expressed the community's appreciation with a plaque on the mall foundation which reads,

"**McGoldrick Aero Mall**
in Recognition of
James P. McGoldrick II
whose dedication to
Spokane Aviation
is unequaled."

CHAPTER 10 – MEMORABILIA AND MISCELLANEOUS

AIRCRAFT OWNERS AND PILOTS ASSOCIATION
ADVANCED MANDATORY NOTICE OF ARRIVALS FOR OVERSEAS TRAVEL

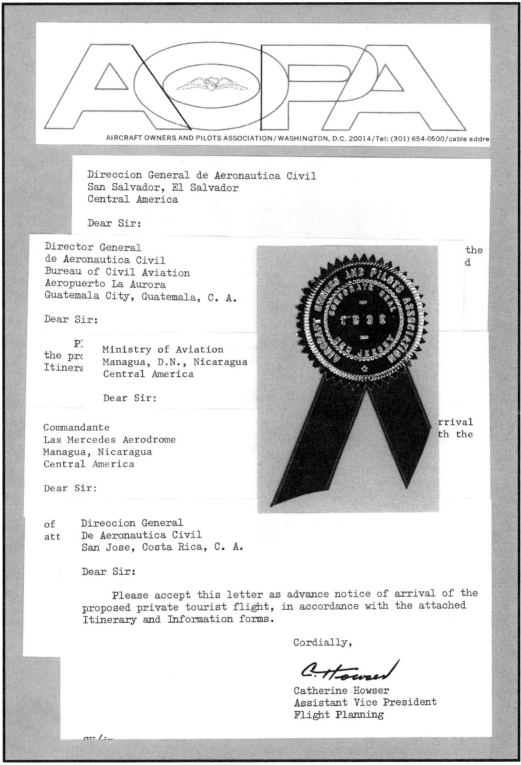

In 1974, when Jim and Milaine flew to Central America, they were required to file flight information with each specific foreign jurisdiction prior to landings. This was coordinated by the AOPA.

. . . foreign travel connections . . .

Oldtime Pilots Share Lore

A group of oldtime pilots from the Spokane area gathered at the Stockyards Inn Friday night to exchange flying stories and to look over books on flying by Steve Mills, left, a Spokane resident and commander of the Washington Civil Air Patrol. At the meeting, Mills gathered information from several of those attending, including James McGoldrick, second from left, Ronald Lamb, center, C. C. Calkins, holding book, and H. R. Wallace, Air Force general, retired, for a book Mills is writing on the history of aviation.

October 27, 1975

GENTLEMEN:

The Association will hold its regular meeting on Monday, November 3, 1975, at the Stockyards Inn beginning at 6:00 p.m. with the cocktail hour and dinner at 7:00 p.m. Please note that we have moved the cocktail hour ahead one half hour.

This meeting will be our annual "OLD TIMERS" night, and we invite everyone to attend -- both old timers and regular pilots. Jim McGoldrick will be Master of Ceremonies. After reminiscence by the old timers, a historical film on flying will be shown.

We hope to see you all next Monday night for our annual "OLD TIMERS" celebration.

A newsclipping and copy of the letter initiating the 1975 Businessmen's Pilots Association meeting at the Stockyards Inn at Spokane. This letter was written by John G. Layman, who was then secretary-treasurer.

CHAPTER 10 – MEMORABILIA AND MISCELLANEOUS

A dinner hosted by the Spokane Businessmen's Pilots Association on November 24, 1975, for a group of "Old Time" pilots. This event took place in the basement of the Stockyards Inn. Inset is Roy Shreck, who died in a plane accident the following year.

A swearing-in ceremony for new members of Spokane's Civil Air Patrol.

. . . old and new aviator friends . . .

JIM McGOLDRICK   SPOKANE AVIATION

OLD TIME PILOTS LIST (1972)
(A few are not pilots but were closely associated with flying)
All addresses are Spokane, Washington, unless otherwise shown. Zip codes were mostly unavailable.

NAME	ADDRESS
Adams, Jim N.	S. 4056 Helena
Anest, Pete	S. 5208 Dearborn
Appling, Dick	E. 11121 - 21st Ave.
Armstrong, Orley	E. 53 Heroy
Baker, Bob	N. 4914 Lacey
Belknap, Burt	S. 4107 Hogan
Blunt, Harry	E. 307 Lacrosse
Brown, Chet	Rockford Bay, Coeur d'Alene, Idaho
Bula, Dean	E. 3133 - 30th
Caldwell, Dr. C. O.	3422 W. Euclid
Calkins, Chuck	c/o Calkins Mfg. Co., Spokane Industrial Park
Cantwell, Wm.	c/o FAA, Felts Field, Spokane, Washington
Carreau, Ernie	E. 2810 - 15th Ave.
Chandler, Charles	Route 1, Greenacres, Washington
Cooney, Vince	E. 808 Longfellow
Connick, Al	N. 4324 Hawthorne
Dean, John	717 E. Rich
Dearborn, Wright	N. 3415 Park Blvd.
Erickson, John	Mead Airport, Mead, Washington
Gardner, Warren	Pines Road-between 10th & 11th (only address known)
Graham, Clarence	4008 N. Howard
Grehan, Frank	S. 1622 McCabe Road
Gural, Art	E. 2605 Thurston
Hagan, Dr. C. E.	S. 1907 Oneida Place
Hall, Emery	E. 10602 Chinook Road
Hansen, Harold	Address unknown - in Seattle now
Hooper, Leroy	Post Falls, Idaho
Johnson, Roy Jr.	E. 136 Rockwood Blvd. (already on BPA list - this is a new address)
Knoles, Irvin	N. 4003 Washington St.
Krous, Virgil	E. 24 Everett
Lamb, Roland	E. 11 Glass
Lampming, Joe	W. 223 Queen
Larned, Harry	S. 3421 Sommer Re., Veradale, Washington
Litzenberger, Carl	Endicott, Washington
Loranger, Joe	c/o Loranger Aviation, Felts Field, Spokane, Washington
Majer, Norm	2415 S. Helena Court
Melius, Lewis	3004 E. 15th Ave.
Miles, Clarence	3628 E. 11th Ave.
Parsons, Bill	W. 1518 Courtland
Pry, Harley	c/o Western Aircraft, Felts Field, Spokane, Washington
Rhodes, Harold	c/o Coeur d'Alene Airport, Coeur d'Alene, Idaho
Roberts, Gene	Route 11, Box 795

. . . more old and new aviator friends . . .

CHAPTER 10 – MEMORABILIA AND MISCELLANEOUS

NAME	ADDRESS
Schimanski, Robert	1014 Club Court
Schmidt, Roy D. W.	2710 Everett
Schirmer, Carl	N. 1141 - 5th St., Coeur d'Alene, Idaho
Seibert, Rene	W. 3427 Walton
Shoemaker, George	E. 735 - 23rd Ave.
Shreck, Roy	Box 1337, Cody, Wyoming
Stevens, Louis	c/o Spokane Falls Community College, Fort Wright
Swinehart, Dr. Paul	E. 44 High Drive
Vandervert, Bob	N. 9917 Waikiki Road
Vordahl, Elmer	E. 12004 - 20th Ave.
Walsh, Bob	E. 17902 Palomino Road, Colbert, Washington
Warner, Jack	E. 11 - 26th Ave.
Warsinske, Al	W. 1741 - 11th Ave.
Wesley, Roy	N. 5739 Driscoll Blvd.
Williams, Frank	2204 W. Pacific, Apt. 5
Younker, Joe	N. 5929 Fotheringham
Veal, Glen	c/o FAA, Felts Field, Spokane, Washington

Old time pilots already BPA members

Alton, Will	Heine, Phil	Swanson, Russ
Anderson, Rod	Husom, Al	Theile, George
Becker, Lew	Johnson, Roy Jr.	Toth, Bill
Butterfield, Mel	Kendall, John	Wallace, H. P. General USAF (Retired)
Calkins, Dwight	McGoldrick, Jim	Walters, Chuck
Gillis, Wilson	Mifflin, John	Warren, Spalding
Heberling, Bob	Robinson, Jim	

Other Old Time Pilots That Were Suggested but Could Not Be Located

Berg, Russ	Gage, Vern	Perry, Hank
Brennan, Kenny	Hagen, Wally	Shuck, Lynn
Carlson, Lloyd	Lyons, Fred	Wilson, Nolan
Cole, Sy Moore, Tom	Wright, Max	

Others Suggested but Unable to Contact Them: (these three were at the old timers meeting last fall)

Brotherton, Bill	Ephrata, Washington
Ebbert, Gordon	Moses Lake, Washington
Larum, Harold	Moses Lake, Washington

Former Civil Air Patrol Cadets that were at the meeting last fall:

Camp, Ron	Moe, Gene
Cooney, Jack	Robbins, Norman, Lt. Col. USAF
	(stationed at Fairchild AFB last fall)

P.S. There are probably many old time pilots in Spokane that are not on this list. This list was compiled about October 15, 1971 by Bill Toth. Some of the addresses may be incorrect by now (September 28, 1972).

. . . and more old and new aviator friends . . .

Jim's friend Warren Gardner, next to his vintage 1929 Golden Eagle Chief NC68N. Warren flew his first plane in 1942 at Wilbur, Washington. His neighbor bought the plane in pieces for his sons. Once the neighbor discovered his sons were not interested in flying, he asked Warren to help him assemble the plane. When together and running, the neighbor asked Warren if he wanted to take it for a spin. Warren loved aviation and had studied every book he could get his hands on. Not telling the neighbor he had never flown before, Warren took the plane to an altitude of about 300 feet. Upon landing, the neighbor asked him if he couldn't go a little higher. Warren took off again for a greater altitude. When he returned, the neighbor asked for a ride. Consequently, Warren flew his first plane and gave his first passenger a ride on the same day. Interestingly, during Warren's lifetime, he has logged 890 hours of flight time. The downside to Warren's aviation career was his inability to ever obtain a pilot's license as he has been blind in one eye for most of his life. He was born with a cataract in his right eye, which was not removed until he turned 75. Warren has spent his lifetime as a logger, several times winning world championship axe-chopping contests. *(Photo courtesy Warren Gardner)*

. . . an accomplished logger friend . . .

WARREN GARDNER
The Logger Pilot

When Warren Gardner bought his Golden Eagle Chief in 1954 for $100 in "as is" condition; the structure had to almost completely rebuilt. Near the end of 1955, Warren had completed the extensive and necessary repairs and made his first test flight, immediately falling in love with the machine. During the many years Warren owned his Golden Eagle, he flew it throughout the entire Northwest.

The Golden Eagle was originally designed by pioneer aviator/mechanic Mark Campbell, who got his start in aviation in 1914. One of the most interesting things about the Golden Eagle is its history. On January 2, 1929, the 18-year-old, destined-to-be-famous aviatrix Bobbi Trout set a world's endurance record (non-refueling) flying a Golden Eagle. She stayed in the air 12 hours and 11 minutes. Less than a month later, this record was broken by Elinor Smith with 13 hours 17 minutes. Not to be outdone, Trout fueled her Golden Eagle with 80 gallons of gas and was able to stay in the air for 17 hours 5 minutes – recapturing the world record. In addition, shortly after that feat, she broke the first woman's night-flying record and also set a women's record for altitude.

Trout set many aviation records, during her lifetime. She was also one of the founding members of the group called the Ninety-Nines, an all-female aviation organization that came into being on November 2, 1929, at Curtiss Field in Valley Stream, Long Island, New York. At the time, there were 117 American female pilots, all invited to assemble for mutual support and the advancement of aviation. Louise Thaden was elected secretary and worked tirelessly to keep the group together as they struggled to organize and grow. In 1931 Amelia Earhart was elected as the group's first president and the group was officially named for the 99 charter members.

Warren Gardner, age 14, with a model E 2 Taylor Cub. Warren's love for flying came at an early age. *(Photo courtesy Warren Gardner)*

Bobbi Trout had an active and full life. In 1976 she received the OX-5 Pioneer Woman of the Year Award. In 1984 she was inducted into the OX-5 Aviation Pioneers Hall of Fame. She was also a former director of Aviation Archives, a California nonprofit corporation dedicated to the preservation of aviation history.

When Lt. Col. Eileen Collins became the first woman to pilot the shuttle into space she took Bobbi's international pilot's license (endorsed by Orville Wright) with her.

On June 24, 1988, Warren Gardner attended a book signing for the book *Just Plane Crazy*, a biography of Bobbi Trout compiled by Carol L. Osburn, an aviation historian. Bobbi, 82 years old at the time, was there for the signing. Since she had set her first world records in a Golden Eagle Chief, she was familiar with Warren's Golden Eagle. She wrote the following:

> 6-24-'88   To Warren Gardner – an early self taught unlicensed pilot, who has flown more hours in our precious Golden Eagle Chief than anyone. What a privilege to meet you and Vivian here at Doctor & Dorothy Fowler's. Best always. Bobbi Trout. (See following page)

Just Plane Crazy

Biography of BOBBI TROUT

by
Donna Veca and Skip Mazzio

As Compiled by:
Carol L. Osborne
Aviation Historian

6-24-'88

To Warren Gardner — an early self taught unlicensed pilot, who has flown more hours in our precious Golden Eagle Chief than anyone. What a privelage to meet you and Vivian here at Doctor + Dorthy Fowler's. Best always.

Bobbi Trout

OSBORNE PUBLISHER, INCORPORATED   1987   Santa Clara, California

This 1928 Boeing 40C 5339, serial number 1043, was delivered to Pacific Air Transport in the summer of 1928 to begin service on Contract Airmail Route (CAM) 8 between Seattle and San Diego. On October 2, 1928, after only five weeks on the line, pilot Grant Donaldson was involved in a tragic crash while flying in bad weather eight miles south of Canyonville, Oregon. Although badly burned, Donaldson survived, but his sole passenger was killed in the accident. This specific aircraft was originally operated by a division of the Boeing Aircraft Company "Pacific Air Transport" between Seattle and San Diego. This is noteworthy as Varney Airlines operated this same type aircraft from Spokane's Felts Field during the late '20s and early '30s. The Boeing 40 aircraft were the first successful commercial aircraft to offer passenger service in the United States.

At the time of the crash, the airplane was carrying a significant number of jewel-quality diamonds. The aircraft was left at the crash sight until the 1990s when the Oregon Aviation Historical Society recovered the remains. In 2000 they sold the remains to Addison Pemberton of Spokane, with the promise from Pemberton to restore and tour the airplane when finished. To date, Pemberton and nine skilled volunteers have spent nearly eight years and 18,000 hours of work restoring this historical treasure, which is scheduled for flight early in 2008. This aircraft is a tribute to the Pacific Northwest and the Boeing Aircraft Company's vision and insight into commercial aviation. It will be the oldest operational Boeing aircraft and the only operational Boeing 40 in the world.

Pemberton and Sons Aviation (Addison Pemberton and family) have been restoring flying antique aircraft for the last 30-plus years. Thus far, they have taken on 18 vintage aircraft projects, truly appreciating their designs and capabilities. Since 1995, they have been based at Felts Field in a 9,000 square foot facility. Their most significant undertaking has been the complete restoration of the above 1928 Boeing 40C. Jim thanks Addison Pemberton for this photo and his contribution to the preservation of Spokane's aviation history.

. . . friends with notable undertakings . . .

The author and two of his three grandsons at the north end of Priest Lake, circa 1976. From left to right: Virgil, Petyr and Jim. Jim's plane was a 1976 Cessna 180-H with EDO 2960 floats.

Milaine McGoldrick and grandson Petyr.

. . . a happy, well-adjusted family . . .

Molly and her pet lion, Lindy. While Milaine and Jim were attending a social hour at the Davenport Hotel, they met and made friends with an officer from the Calgary (Canada) Zoo. They learned the lion cubs were part of a petting zoo for children. Once they reached a certain age, they were put out to individuals for a while until matured, at which time they had to be returned to the zoo in Calgary. A month later, Milaine received a surprise telephone call from the zoo official offering the loan of a lion cub. Milaine talked a family friend, Chuck Walters, into flying her to Calgary in his Bonanza, to pick the club up and fly back to Spokane to surprise Jim with the new member of the family. When the U.S. customs officer met them at Felts Field, he asked, "and what do you have today Chuck?" He answered, "An 80-pound lion cub in the back seat." Soon word passed around the neighborhood as kids all wanted to see Lindy the lion. After a short time, the McGoldricks' insurance carrier called, ending Lindy's stay with the McGoldrick family. Fortunately, a local veterinarian had been looking for such a prize and Lindy had a new home. According to Jim, "That ended the lion episode – thank God."

Molly graduated from the University of Washington, experiencing her junior year at the University of Vienna as an exchange student. She also received her master's degree in forestry and started her own company, Northwest Arborvitae. She was a consulting arborist and urban forester.

. . . a beautiful daughter and Lindy her pet lion . . .

Mikki was under contract to Warner Brothers in Hollywood after attending Pasadena Playhouse, an educational institution for theatrical knowledge and drama. She had a very interesting career in movies and television and is still a voting member of the Screen Actors Guild for the annual Academy Awards. Mikki lives in Spokane with her husband, John Rovtar, and loves the summers at Coeur d'Alene and Pend Oreille lakes. She was named Warner Brothers' Ingenue of the Year and represented them in the Deb-Star Ball, where the above photo was taken. Insets: Mikki's son and our #3 grandson Jaimie and Mikki's wedding photo.

. . . another beautiful daughter . . .

. . . nice gifts and a happy wife.

Those are just some of the good things that come to old Fudpucker aviators.

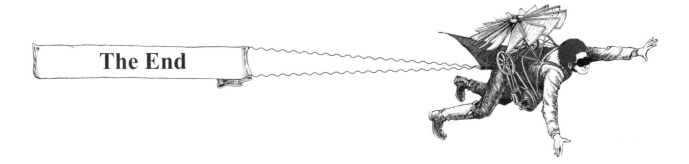

INDEX

A

Accidents, *see* Crashes; Forced landings; Fatalities
Adams, Chuck, 148
Aerial photography, 26, 35, 42, 77, 133, 190-191, *See also* Felts Field, Aerial photographs of
Aero: America's Aviation Weekly, 14
Aero Club of America, 11, 15
Aero Club of Spokane, 198, 204
Aeronca aircraft, 195
Afro-American pilots, *See* Black pilots
Air beacons, *See* Beacons; Fancher Beacon
Air circus, 34, 67-69
Air Commerce Act, 162
Air Derby Association, 88, 148
Air mapping, 190-191
Air races, *See* National Air Derby and Air Races; Women's air races
Air shows, 1-9, 98, 193, *See also* Air circus; National Air Derby and Air Races
Airlines, *See* Passenger Service; Northwest Airlines; Varney Airlines, etc.
Airmail service, 140, 144, 161, 164, 168
Airplane-automobile races, 4, 9, 20-21
Airplane dealerships, 36, 53, 134, 143, 144, 174, 206
Airplane interiors, 124, 135, 154
Airplane manufacture and repair, 21, 39, 52, 59, 176-178, 181, 191
Airports, 35-36, 38-41, 50, 56, 70, 168, 206, 208, *See also* names of individual airports, e.g. Felts Field; Parkwater, etc.
Albert, Lawrence, 56
Albi, Joe, 208
Alexander Eaglerock Company, *See* Inland Eaglerock Sales Company
All Women's Air Frolic, *See* Women's air races
Allen, Bud, 19

Allenberg, Jack, 56, 98, 148
Altitude record in Spokane (1920), 38
Anderson, Edna Barrie, 203
Anderson, Eric H. 164-166
Anzani engine, 21-22, 36
Arctic Patrol/Arctic Flyers, 158, 160
Army Air Corps, 158
Arneson, Arthur, 21-22
Aston, Thomas G., 89
Automobile-airplane races, *See* Airplane-automobile races
Avey, John A., 67-70
Aviation schools, *See* Flight instruction
Axberg, Edward, 56, 78

B

B & L Flying Service, *See* Burns and Lamb
Babcock, Don, 89
Balanca aircraft, 178
Ballough, Eddie, 118
Barnard, Nathan N. "Nat", 35, 37-38, 51
Barnard, William T. "Bill", 25, 35-39, 43-44, 51, 59
Barnstorming and stunt flying, 18-20, 34-35, 46, 90-91, 118, 203, *See also* Air circus; Doolittle, Jimmy; Hamilton, Charles
Batten, Eugene, 112
Beacons, 98-99, 169
Beech aircraft
Bennett, Floyd
Bigelow, Edgar, 56
Bigelow Johnson Aviation Company, 142, 174, 176, 180, 192, 194, 201
Biplanes, 9, 11, 22, 101, 106, 122, 206, *See also* Curtiss biplane; Jenny; Lincoln-Standard, etc.
Black pilots, 206-208
Bluebird aircraft, *See under* Curtiss

Boeing aircraft/Boeing Company, 79, 114, 144, 163, 166, 167, 229
Bomb demonstrations, 98
Bonanza aircraft, 183
Bootlegging, 56, 199
Bortles, Ira, 182
Boyles, Leon, 89, 148
Breen, Major, 58
Breese, Vance, 128
Brinnon, Kenneth, 195, 196
Brittin, L. H., 201
Brooks, Leo, 89
Brookwalter, Verne, 150, 153
Brown, Bill, 176, 178
Brown, Thoburn and Bill, 176, 178
Brown Industries, 176-178
Brown Metalplane Company, 177
Budd, Herbert L., 176
Buhl aircraft, 46, 94, 119, 134, 135, 138, 142-144, 162, 193, *See also Spokane Sun-God*
Burch, Arthur, Mayor, 203
Burgess-Wright aircraft, 11
Burns, Homer, 193-194
Burns & Lamb Co., 193-194
Buroker, Gladys Dawson, 203
Burrow, William, 89
Businessmen's Pilots Association, *See* Spokane Businessmen's Pilots Association

C

Calkins Air Terminal, 180, 206
Calkins, Claude, 180, 205, 222
Calkins, Dwight, 195, 205
Camp Earl Hoisington, See Earl Hoisington Field
Campbell, Kenneth, 24
Campbell, O. A., 24
Carroll, Ray, 88
Cascade Mountains, 35
Cessna aircraft, 209, 230
Civil Aeronautics Authority/Administration, 176

Civil Works Administration, 168
Civilian Pilot Training Program, 182, 194, 203, 206-207
Clifton, Jack, 195
Coeur d'Alene (lake and city), 43-44, 188
Connick, Al, 19, 35, 39, 43, 67-68, 135, 168, 180, 193
Connick Air Service, 193
Continental Divide, 11-13
Cooper, Byron, 56
Coppula, Alphonse "Al", 94, 104, 117, 150, 153, 193
Corrigan, Kathleen, 183
Cowles, William H., 55, 89, 95, 148
Craney, Ed, 57
Crashes, 49, 65, 81, 130-131, 176, 182-183, 186, 188-189, 196, 199, 203; *See also* Fatalities; Forced landings; Government regulation; Itinerant pilots
Cuddeback, Leon D., 164
Culbertson, Frank, 89, 96
Cunningham, Vera (McDonald), 94, 98, 109
Curtiss, Glenn H. 6-7
Curtiss aircraft and engines, 14, 20, 138, 142
    Biplane, 1, 3-8, 11, 34, 112
    Bluebird, 36, 42
    Hawk, 90, 113-115, 118, 120, 158, 174
    Jenny, 24-25, 35-38, 42, 60, 67, 70
    Oriole, 33, 38, 121
    OX-5, 24-25, 35, 46, 50, 138, 142, 176, 227
    Pusher-type, 11, 17-18
    Seagull, 42-44

D

Dahl, Ray, 89
Daniels, Ralph, 138
Davenport, Louis, 89, 96
Davenport Hotel, 84-86, 96, 99, 201
Davies, Frank, 89
Dean, John, 176

De Burger, Louis Norman, 136, 138, 140-141, 146-147
De Haviland aircraft, 25, 53, 60-61, 64, 67, 69, 71, 76
Dessert, Vic, 69, 89, 95, 139, 148, 152, 154, 208
Dirigibles, 10, 24, 70
Dixon, Cromwell, Jr., 11-16
Doolittle, Jimmy, 90-91, 116, 118
Doran, John "Jack", 39
Douglas aircraft, 76, 82, 170
Dunlap, Kenneth, 136, 138

E

Eaglerock airplanes, 174, 176
Eaglerock Co., *See* Inland Eaglerock Sales Company
Eaker, Ira, 152
Earhart, Amelia, 201-202
Earl Hoisington Field, 56-57, 68
Electra airliner, 167
Enarson, Arthur G., 136, 138
Endurance flights, *See* S*pokane Sun-God*
Evans, Walter, 89, 117

F

Fairchild aircraft, 182, 191, 203, 206
Fairgrounds, *See* Spokane Interstate Fairgrounds
Falcon aircraft, 72
Fancher, John "Jack"
    World War I, 25, 98-99
    Washington Air National Guard, 54-57, 64, 69, 78, 98
    and Lindbergh, 85, 87
    1927 National Air Races, 88-89, 95, 98, 102
    Death and memorials, 98-100
Fancher Beacon, 99
Farbro, Tom, 193
Fatalities, 12, 16, 43-44, 67-72, 98-101, 136, 138, 141, 146-147, 187, 192-193, 229

Federal Aviation Agency, 49
Felts, James Buell, 55-56, 71-72
Felts Field, 40-41, 50, 85, 87, 145, 157, 169
    Named for James Buell Felts, 72
    Administration/Terminal Building, 166, 168, 170
    Aerial photographs of, 59, 68, 111-112, 145, 157, 167, 169, 179-180
    Hangars, 48, 51, 59, 62, 168-169, 174, 176, 179, 191
    Mamer Memorial Clock, 170-171
    See also Earl Hoisington Field; Parkwater; National Air Derby and Air Races; Spokane Airways; *Spokane Sun-God*, etc.
Fetters, J. M., 35, 37
First aerial moving picture of Spokane, 35
First African American in Spokane to earn pilot's license, 206
First air show in Spokane, 1-9
First airplane crossing of Cascade Mountains 35
First airplane crossing of Continental Divide 11-13
First airplane dealership in Spokane, 36
First fair in Spokane, 10
First fatality at Parkwater, 67
First flight in Spokane, 1-9
First post-World War I aviation activity in Spokane, 33-34
First seaplane in the Inland Northwest, 42
First tractor monoplane built in Spokane, 22
Fish, Shirley, 203
Fixed base operators, 49, 135, 168
Fleming, Charles, Mayor, 24, 85, 87
Flight attendants, 205
Flight exhibitions, *see* Air circus; Air shows; Barnstorming and stunt flying
Flight instruction, 14, 17, 37, 135, 137-138, 182, 194-194; *See also* Civilian Pilot Training Program; Women pilots

Float planes, *See* Seaplanes
Flood, Ed, 89, 96
Flying circus, *See* Air circus
Fokker aircraft, 25, 34, 66, 134, 152, 156
Forced landings, 37, 70, 138
Ford aircraft, 94, 96, 133-134, 136, 138-139, 141-142, 167, 201; *See also* Tin Goose; *West Wind I & II*
Ford, Jim, 89, 162, 208
Forest fire patrol, 49, 64-65, 71
Foster Russell Airport, *See* Russell-Symons
Frances, Paul, 36
French, Ellsworth C., 56, 89, 96, 125, 148, 171
Freng, Ragnar, 69
Fried, Marcella, 195, 204
Fudpucker World Airlines, 210-214
Fuel, 139, 148, *See also* Refueling in flight

G

Gardner, Warren, 226-228
Garnett, P. J. "Phil", 89, 96, 142, 208
Geiger Field, 207
Gephart, Valentine, 175
Gleason, Dick, 56
Glover Field, 18-20, 22
Goddard, Norman, 122
Goetz, Harry, 148
Golden Eagle Chief, 226-227
Government regulation and agencies, 35, 49, 166, 167, 169, 176; *See also* Pilot's licenses
Graham, John W., 89, 96
Graham, L. B., 57
Green, Harry, 4, 6
Grombacher, Ray, 89, 96
Gypsy (plane) 122
Gypsy pilots, *See* Itinerant pilots

H

Hagin, Wally, 206-208
Hahn, Harold, 44, 58, 191
Hairiston, Bob, 195
Hall Scott engines, 47
Halladay, Besse, 203
Hamilton, Charles K., 1-9
Hamilton, Tom, 128
Hamilton aircraft, 94, 105, 128, 167-168, 191
Hanson, Harold, 188-189
Hardesty, Lloyd, 193
Hartley, Roland, Governor, 55, 67, 69, 85
Hartnett, Clare A., 176, 201
Harvey, Earl O., 24
Harvey-Campbell Dirigible Aircraft Corporation, 24
Hawk aircraft, *See under* Curtiss
Haynes, C. V., 58, 88, 138, 148, 190
Heath, Rex, 136, 138, 141
Heath Parasol aircraft, 94, 120
Hebberd, Charles, 89, 95, 148
Heflin, Alma, 201, 203
Henry, George, 55, 67
Hicks, Sam, 55-56
Hill, Lloyd, 89
Hisso aircraft and engines, 50, 56, 67, 75, 132
Hoisington Field, *See* Earl Hoisington Field
Holman, Charles W. "Speed", 94, 110, 120
Holter, Charles, 78, 188, 189
Hoover, Herbert, President, 156
Hughes, Howard, 169
Hurtig, Lew, 42
Hutchinson, Louise Prugh, 203
Hutton, Levi, 22
Hydro aircraft, 11

I

Inland Eaglerock Sales Company, 174
International Air Transport Company, 137
Interstate Fairgrounds, *See* Spokane Interstate Fairgrounds
Itinerant pilots, 49

J

"Jenny" aircraft, *See under* Curtiss
Johnson, Clyde, 89
Johnson, H. W., *See* Bigelow Johnson Aviation Company
Jones, Harold, 208
Jones, Milaine, *See* McGoldrick, Milaine Jones

K

Kemmery, Bert, 14, 17, 21
Kessel, Owen, 35
Klopp, Henry, 164

L

Laird aircraft, 110, 118
Lamb, Roland, 193-195, 222
Lamb Flying Service, 194-195, 204, *See also* Burns & Lamb Company
Landa, Jean Smith, 203
Landry, Arnold, 193
Langley, Elmer E., 78
Le Beau, Eddie, *See* Rose, Jack
Le Blonde engine, 176
Le Masters, Eustus, 208
Levitch, Oscar, 149
Libby, Charles/Libby Studio, 38, 88, 132
Liberty Lake, 38, 42
Licenses, *See* Pilot's licenses
Lincoln-Standard aircraft, 36, 43, 47, 51
Lindbergh, Charles, 83-87
Lloyd, Glenwood and Stanley, 19
Lockheed aircraft, 166-167, 169, 182
Luscombe aircraft, 182, 195, 199, 206

M

Magin, Louis, Reverend, 69
Mail service, *See* Airmail service
Malstrom, Einar, 56
Mamer, Fay, 171, 173
Mamer, Nicholas Bernard "Nick", 19, 42, 44-47, 70, 135, 142, 149, 180, 193, 199-200
    World War I service, 45, 173
    Barnstorming/stunting, 43
    Air National Guard connection, 57-58, 64, 72, 171-173
    Forest fire patrol, 49, 64
    National Air Races, 88, 94, 119
    Safest pilot, 46
    Pilot for Northwest, 166-168, 170, 178, 191
    Death and memorials, 170-173
    See also Spokane Sun-God
Mamer Air Transport/Mamer Flying Service, 48, 133-134, 137, 140-145, 168, 201
Mamer Memorial Clock, 170-171
Mamer-Shreck Co., 178, 181-182
Martin, Clarence, Governor, 79, 166, 171
Martin, M. B., 38
Matthews, Dave, 38, 51
Matthews, T. D., 38
McClaine, Maude B., 199, 200, 201
McClellan, R. C., 17, 35
McCroskey, Floyd, 25
McDonald, Bruce, 88, 94, 119
McGoldrick, A. E., "Ed", 24
McGoldrick, James Patrick, v
McGoldrick, James Patrick II "Jim", v, 209, 216-217, 221-222
    Childhood memories of Spokane aviation, 84, 90-91, 94, 100-101, 136, 138, 158-159, 162, 165-166, 174
    Education/athletics, v, 195
    Flight instruction, v, 138, 195
    Courtship and marriage, 195, 206
    Business, v
    Family, 209, 230-233
    Friendships, 25, 43, 56-57, 68, 95-96, 134, 195, 226; *See also* Old Time Pilots
    Aviation activities and honors, v, 39, 209, 215-218, 220

Fudpucker World Airlines, 210-214
McGoldrick, Milaine (Jones), 166, 195-199, 204, 209
McGoldrick, Milton, 24-25, 37, 39, 46, 89-90, 96, 139, 166
McGoldrick Lumber Company, 46, 90, 96, 129, 33, 164
McPherson, E. S., "Eddie", 89, 98
Messer, Claude H., 42-43
Metalark aircraft, 176-178
Meyers, Charlie, 117
Miller, Joe, 192
Miller, John, 128
Miss Spokane (Marguerite Motie), 34
Miss Spokane (plane), 34
Miss Veedol, 126
Mitchell, D. R., 136, 138
Mitchell, S. A. 89
Model airplanes, 174, 176, 227
Modern Automobile and Tractor School, 43-44, 46, 51
Monaghan, Betty, 195, 204
Monroe Street Bridge, 18-19
Motie, Marguerite, 34
Myring, Gene, 178

N

National Aeronautics Association, 157
National Air Derby and Air Races, Spokane, 85-98
    Spokane boosters and publicity, 88-89, 91 93, 95-98, 124-125, 132
    Prizes and winners, 88, 90, 93-94, 97, 102 105, 109-110, 112, 117-119
    Jimmy Doolittle, 90-91, 116, 118
    Statistics, 94-95
National Air Derby Association, *See* Air Derby Association
National Guard Aviation Unit, *See* Washington Air National Guard
Neely, Harold R., 56-57, 78, 89

Newman Lake, 158-159
Night flying, 99, 169
Ninety-Nines, 201, 203, 227
Nonstop flights, *See* National Air Derby and Air Races; Spokane Sun-God
Norge (dirigible), 70
Northern tier route, 134, 140, 162, 169
Northwest Aircraft Company, 34-35
Northwest Airways/Airlines, 140, 162-163, 166 170, 178, 201, 219
Northwest Aviation Company, 161
Northwest Electronics, Inc., v
Nyrop, Donald W., 219

O

Observation Squadron, *See* Washington Air National Guard
O'Connell, Neal, 150, 153
Old Time Pilots Club, 67, 70, 182, 222-225
Oldfield, Barney, 20, 22
Orien aircraft, 168
Oriole aircraft, *See under* Curtiss
Owen, Claude, 56, 78
Owen, Robert W., 55-56, 70, 78, 148
Owen, Russell E. "Russ", 163, 191-192
OX-5, *See under* Curtiss; WACO

P

Packard aircraft, 116, 121
Pangborn, Clyde, 34-35
Parachute jumping, 123, 195-198
Parkwater, 17, 34-39, 50-51, 53, 68, 71, *See also* Earl Hoisington Field; Felts Field
Partlow, Carl, 56
Passenger service, 34-35, 37-38, 134-135, 161 169, *See also* Northwest; Varney; etc.
Pattee, Glen, 89
Paulsen, Clarence I. "Cip", 96, 135-136, 168, 178, 180
Pedicord, George W., 100-101

Pemberton, Addison/Pemberton and Sons Aviation, 229
Peters, Harold , 78, 80
Peters, Marcus, 80
Peyton, Harlan, 85, 89, 95
Pierong, Harry W. "Nick", 89, 96-97, 148
Pilot's licenses, 11, 15, 195, 200-201, 227
Pilots, Unlicensed, 226-228
Piper Aircraft Company, 201
Porterfield aircraft, 194
Powder Puff Derby, 201
Pratt and Whitney engines, 166
Priestley, Schuyler, 67-70
Prison labor in building airstrips, 39
PT-1 aircraft, 72
Pursuit planes, 114, 158-160 See also Curtiss Hawk

Q

Quesada, Elwood, 152
Question Mark (plane), 152-156

R

Races between airplanes and automobiles, See Airplane-automobile races
Radio communication, 57, 99, 169
Ralston, J. C., 162
Rankin, Tex, 91, 118
Refueling in flight, 150-154, 156, 158
Rexroad, Captain, 69
Riddle, W. B., 24
Robertson, Alyce, 195, 204
Robertson, Edward W., 99, 171
Roosevelt, Franklin D., President, 166-167
Rose, Jack, 56, 65, 138
Routes, 169, 201; *See also* Northern tier route
Royal Windsor, 127
Russell, Foster and airport, 38-39, 42-43
Russell-Symons Aviation Co. and airport, 36, 38 39

Rutter, R. I., 55, 95, 171
Ryan aircraft, 48, 94, 124, 130, 138, 142, 150, 153

S

Safety, *See* Accidents; Crashes; Fatalities; Government regulation; Itinerant pilots
Sartori, Dorothy, 203
Schafhausen, Ann, 213
Schafhausen, John, 213
Schiller, "Duke", 127
Schirmer, Carl, 175-176, 191
Seagull aircraft, *See under* Curtiss aircraft
Seaplanes, 42-45, 178, 195, 209, 230
Selfridge Field, Michigan, Pursuit Squadron, 158 160
Semple, Charlotte, 195
Shackleton, Ralph, 193
Sherman, Lawrence, 55-57, 68-69, 78, 138, 190
Shinn, Millie, 203
Shreck, Roy, 182-187, 193, 205, 223
Shrock, Ray, 56
Simpson, John, 58
Smith, Daisy, 196, 199
Smith, Dwight, 56, 67, 70
Spaatz, T., 152
Spokane Air Races and Air Derby, *See* National Air Races and Air Derby
Spokane Airways, 135-136, 138, 140-142, 144, 148
Spokane Aviation Company, 36, 38, 43-44, 51
Spokane Businessmen's Pilots Association, 222, 223
Spokane Chamber of Commerce, 88, 94, 162
   Aviation Committee, v, 17, 39, 208
Spokane Civil Air Patrol, 223
Spokane Flying Club, 35, 201
Spokane Interstate Fairgrounds, 1-2, 8-11, 35, 46, 84, 142
Spokane Ministerial Association, 67
Spokane Sun-God, 143, 148-157

Sponsorship and promotion, 148
Route, 150
Christening/Indians present, 151
Refueling in flight, 150-154, 156, 158
Plane to ground communication, 152-154
Supplies, 156
Achievements and statistics, 156
Telegram from President Herbert Hoover, 156
Stearman aircraft, 65, 162-163, 166, 182, 193, 196
Stimson, Art, 61
Stinson, Eddie, 126
Stinson aircraft, 126-128, 135, 182
Stout, William B./Stout Metal Airplane Company, 134
Stunt flying, See Barnstorming and stunt flying; Air circus
Sun-God, See *Spokane Sun-God*
Sunset Airport, 206, 208
Super Airport, See Sunset Airport; Geiger Field
Swallow aircraft, 88, 164
Swineheart, Paul, 17, 18
Symons, Tom, 25, 36, 38-39, 42, 55-56, 94, 104, 117
Symons-Russell Aviation Company, See Russell Symons Aviation Co./Airport

T

Taylor aircraft, 182, 194, 227
Texaco Company, 148, 152
Thompson, De Lloyd, 20, 22
Thompson, Maurice, 55-57
Tin Goose, 133-145
Toombes, Guy, 89, 96
Toth, Bill, 43, 67, 70, 182
Towne, Mary, 203
Trans-oceanic flight, 34-35, 83, 126-127
Trout, Bobbi, 227-228

U

Ude, W. H., 89

United Aircraft, 116
United Airlines, 161, 163-164, 166, 168-169
United States Aircraft Corporation, 42, 44, 51-52

V

Vandervert, Bob, 195
Varney, Walter T., 164
Varney Airlines, 161-164, 166, 229
Vintage airplanes, 226-229

W

WACO aircraft, 46, 117-118
Wadsworth, W., 55, 78, 138, 148
Wakefield, Newton "Newt", 135, 137
Walker, Art, 148, 153, 155, 157
Wallace, Hillford R., 17, 19, 43-45, 55-56, 78, 81, 39, 208, 216-217, 222
Biography, 25-26
Air National Guard, 26, 58, 81, 173, 190, 204
Civilian aviation work, 44, 176, 190-191
Wallace Aerial Surveys, 26, 191
Wallace Aero Institute, 190
Wallace Aeromotive Company, 44, 176
Wallace Air/Flying Service, 176, 190-191
Warren, Felix, 164
Washington Air National Guard/116th Observation Squadron, 26, 38, 51, 54-83, 97, 101, 104, 136-138, 145, 168-169, 171, 176, 190
Fancher first commander 55-56, 64; *See also* Fancher, John
Original 13 officers, 55-56
Earl Hoisington Field headquarters, 56, 58-59
Radio communication, 57
Air circus, 1925, 64, 67-70
Aircraft upgraded, 72-78
Mamer Memorial Ceremony, 171, 173
See also National Air Derby and Air Races
Wasmer, Louis, 134-135, 168, 180, 206
Wasp engines, 191
WASPS (Women Air Force Service Pilots), 203

Weather service flights, 182
Webster, Stanley, Judge, 39
Wenatchee, 35, 98
West Wind I and II, 133, 140, 142, 144, 145
White Pine Sash Company, 164
Whitman, Jean, 203
Wiley, Frank, 151
Williams, Al, 91
Williams, William H., 55-56, 136, 138-139, 140, 141, 146-147
Wilson, Bob, 150, 153
Wilson, Sam, 139-140, 146-147
Wirt, Ed, 25
Women Air Force Service Pilots, *See* WASPS
Women pilots, 195-205, 227-228
Women's air races, 201, 203
Woodring, Irvin, 94, 115

Works Progress Administration, 169, 208
World War I, 23-32
    Aircraft, 23-24, 32
    Recruitment, 27-31
    Spokane area flyers, 25-26, 98-99, 192
World War II, *See* Civilian Pilot Training Program; WASPS
Wright aircraft and ngines, 50, 65, 76, 94, 110, 133, 144, 148, 153
Wylie, Deb, 17, 39

Y
Youngest licensed pilot, 11, 15

Z
Zephyr aircraft, *See* Lockheed aircraft

JIM McGOLDRICK – SPOKANE AVIATION